BREADS, ROLLS, AND PASTRIES

The Flavor of New England

BREADS, ROLLS, AND PASTRIES

YANKEE, INC.
Dublin, New Hampshire

Edited by Georgia Orcutt and Sandra Taylor
Designed By Carl Kirkpatrick
Illustrated by Pamela Carroll

Yankee, Inc., Dublin, New Hampshire 03444

First Edition

Library of Congress Catalog Card No. 81-50147

ISBN 0-911658-28-9

Contents

Introduction

Many real estate agents will tell you, partly in jest and partly in earnest, that if you want to sell your house, have bread baking in the oven whenever a prospective buyer walks in the door. I tried this once and it worked, and I've never since doubted the power of yeast.

Baking bread, and then eating it, is one of the fine, simple pleasures in life — although it is often considered a luxury today, especially in this weight-conscious era. But as recently as 40 years ago, freshly baked breads and pastries were a part of everyday life in New England, as well as in most of America. The history of bread-making in New England goes back much further, of course, to corn breads made in hot cast-iron pans, fragrant brown breads steamed in kettles, white breads baked six and eight loaves at a time, and delicious, exotic holiday breads from ethnic communities both north and south.

Today, baking has been simplified by the availability of packaged, pre-measured yeast and ready-to-use flour. Food processors and electric mixers reduce the labors of stirring and kneading. And our predictable modern ovens heat quickly and evenly to take the guessing out of baking. As a result, a world of fine breads, rolls, and pastries is within any cook's reach, and this book has been compiled to put you in touch with most of them.

The weekend chef who views baking as a relaxing change of pace from a hectic workweek will find multi-step yeast breads, and challenges such as croissants and salt-rising bread. The everyday baker who rarely has time between meals to take on elaborate productions can choose from dozens of easy batter breads, biscuits, and muffins. And for those who make a special meal out of Sunday breakfast, or who like to rise early and make breakfast an occasion, there are also suggestions for waffles, doughnuts, fritters, and coffee cakes.

Whether you are selling your house, entertaining friends, or simply playing in the kitchen, there is no time like the present to start baking.

Georgia Orcutt

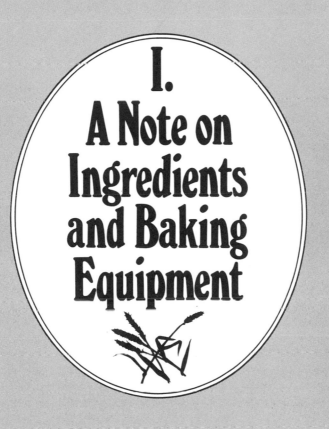

I.
A Note on Ingredients and Baking Equipment

Even the most inexperienced baker can enjoy the pleasure of bread fresh from the oven. With few exceptions, the recipes chosen for this book do not require special skills. Proper ingredients, self-confidence, and a little patience are all you need.

As you experiment with a variety of breads, you will quickly come to appreciate their flexibility. If you do not have the exact ingredients a recipe suggests, you can improvise by making substitutions (see page 14 for examples) or by simply working with what is at hand.

FLOURS

Unless otherwise indicated, the recipes in this book have been tested with all-purpose white flour. However, this does not mean you cannot use other flours, such as rye, whole wheat, hard wheat (the professional baker's favorite), graham, barley, rice, and buckwheat. Try each kind, as they all vary in the amount of liquid they will absorb. Bread flour, marked as such, is hard to find, but it absorbs more moisture than most other flours and makes a wonderful, close-textured loaf.

Breads that are made with white flour, or half white and half whole wheat, will be the lightest in color and texture. For breads that are heavier, coarser, and darker colored, omit all white flour and use only whole wheat or a mixture of less-refined flours; then let the bread rise only once, in loaf pans, before baking.

Bran, oatmeal, and other hot and cold cereals can be added to the bread dough along with or in place of some flour to provide yet another change in taste or texture.

Precise measurements of flour cannot be given for all bread recipes. The amounts listed with each of the yeast breads are approximations. If the dough is sticky after the recommended measurement of flour has been used, add more flour, one-quarter to one-half cup at a time, until the dough can be easily handled. Knead well and add even more flour if necessary. Dough that has the proper amount of flour kneaded into it will feel elastic and smooth.

YEAST

If you have access to fresh yeast, which some bakers claim gives bread a sweeter flavor and better "nose" than packaged dry yeast, proof it before completing the recipe: dissolve the yeast in one-quarter to one-half cup warm (80° to 90°) water, add a pinch of sugar, and set aside in a warm place. The yeast is working and ready to use if it bubbles and begins to swell in 15 minutes. If there is no sign of activity, discard it.

Fresh yeast will keep for two weeks in the refrigerator, up to two months in the freezer. Half an ounce of fresh yeast equals one package of dry yeast.

Since fresh yeast is virtually impossible to find in most areas, the recipes included here call for dry yeast. Packages of dry yeast are stamped with a date giving their shelf life. There is no need to test or proof this yeast if it has been stored in a cool place such as the refrigerator.

Dry yeast should be dissolved in slightly warmer liquid (100° to 115°) than is fresh yeast, but be sure the liquid is not *too* warm since high temperatures can destroy the yeast's action.

YEAST BREADS

Yeast gives bread a distinct flavor and makes it rise. And because it is possible to add or alter numerous ingredients — thereby developing unusual flavors and textures — yeast breads can be creative endeavors.

There is no magic to the amount of yeast used in making one or several loaves of bread. In general, recipes using four or fewer cups of flour can be made with one-half to one package of dry yeast; recipes made with four to ten cups of flour require one to three packages. The amount of yeast used as well as the temperature of the other ingredients called for will determine how quickly the dough rises. For best results, bring bread ingredients to room temperature before using.

Yeast breads are generally kneaded, which assures that the yeast is evenly mixed through the dough. If you skimp on this important step, your bread may turn out heavy and too moist.

Knead dough on a floured board or on a floured cloth that is well secured to a tabletop.

There are many ways to knead bread, and most bakers develop their own techniques. Use the heel of one hand for pushing and fold the dough over with the other hand; or use both hands — pushing, folding, and then rotating the dough a quarter turn, and repeating the process. If you have an electric mixer with a dough hook, use this for your initial mixing and kneading, and finish with several minutes of hand-kneading.

When kneading bread, gradually add enough flour to form a dough that is pliable but not sticky, as described earlier. Then place the dough in a buttered bowl and turn it so that the entire surface area is well greased. This will keep a crust from forming prematurely and prevent the dough from drying out.

Cover the bowl with a clean towel or plastic wrap and place in a warm spot to rise. Generally it takes one and a half to two hours for bread to rise at a room temperature of 75° to 85°. For yeast to work best, the bowl should stand in a draft-free place. An electric oven turned on low, gas oven with pilot light, radiator, sunny windowsill, and top of the refrigerator are a few of the many possible locations to try.

In a very cold room, set the bowl of dough over a kettle of hot water (double-boiler fashion) and bundle the bowl and kettle in blankets or thick towels. Renew the water as necessary to provide continual warmth to the dough.

To determine whether bread dough has risen to an adequate stage, try this simple test. Quickly press a fingertip into the surface of the dough. If a dent remains, the dough has risen long enough.

If your breadmaking is interrupted, or if you can't wait several hours for bread to rise, slow down the action of the yeast by refrigerating the dough. This will not adversely affect the final product.

To stretch your baking out over several days, as a busy schedule may demand, make any recipe using yeast, but increase the measure of yeast by one half; let the kneaded dough sit in a warm place for about 15 minutes, then cover, and refrigerate overnight or all day. Remove from the refrigerator, punch down the dough, and proceed with the recipe. Or, if a second rising is required, put dough in a warm place for about ten minutes, then refrigerate again until adequately risen.

When the dough is ready to be baked, press it into a greased loaf pan, or, if there's a large amount, divide it equally among two or more pans. If you wish to shape kneaded dough into a loaf, roll it out with the palms of your hands into a thick cylinder or rope-like shape. Fold this into thirds, pinching edges gently together, and place seam-side down in a greased loaf pan. Or, for a round, free-form loaf, roll the dough into a ball, pat the top to flatten it slightly, and place on a greased baking sheet.

Generally bread dough is allowed to rise again after it is shaped into a loaf or transferred to a bread pan. Before baking it, you might wish to brush the dough with a mixture either of egg white and water, which gives the crust a shine without browning, or of egg yolk and cream or milk, which makes the crust brown and shiny.

You can tell whether a loaf of bread has baked long enough by tapping on the bottom of the pan; if it sounds hollow, the bread is done. If the bread is darker than desired when removed from the oven, brush it with melted butter to soften the crust.

Allow bread that has finished baking to cool for only a few minutes in its pan, then turn out onto a bread rack for the remainder of the cooling time. Otherwise, the heat from the bread pan will make the bottom of the loaf soggy.

Do not try to slice a loaf of bread while it is still hot. Let it cool at least an hour, sometimes longer, then cut it with a knife with a serrated edge.

QUICK BREADS, BATTER BREADS, AND BREAKFAST PASTRIES

A slightly different set of rules applies to these breads. Measurements of ingredients are more important here than with yeast breads. Too much or too little flour, inadequate liquid, or improper seasoning can spell disaster, not innovation.

To change the taste and texture of the bread, keep measurements the same, but feel free to substitute different liquids (orange, cranberry, or lemon juice, for example) and different dry ingredients (chopped nuts, lemon peel, candied fruits, raisins, currants, cranberries, etc.).

These breads should pull away from the sides of their pans and feel springy to the touch when they have finished baking. Or, a toothpick inserted in the center that comes out clean also indicates that the bread is done.

Serve quick breads when they have completely cooled. Moist batter breads should sit overnight before they are served; this makes slicing easier and sometimes even enhances their flavor.

When making muffins, pancakes, or waffles, use an ice cream scoop or ladle for transferring the batter from bowl to pan or griddle. If a section of a greased muffin pan is left empty, fill it with water so it won't burn during baking. Cast-iron muffin pans give baked goods an even crust, but since they are slow to heat, they should be placed in the oven as it preheats.

Muffins, biscuits, and rolls made without yeast should be eaten minutes after being removed from the oven. They do not improve with age.

For frying doughnuts, crullers, and fritters, use lard or vegetable shortening that has been heated in a heavy pan to about 370°. If you don't have a thermometer, drop a chunk of dry bread into the fat; it is hot enough for frying when the bread cube sizzles, browns, and rises to the top in about one minute. If the fat is not hot enough, the fried product will turn out to be very greasy.

SUBSTITUTIONS

As already discussed, there is never just one way to make any bread, and as a result, the variety of finished products is endless. Making a simple change such as using currants instead of raisins, omitting or adding nuts, or using milk instead of water alters the taste and texture of a bread. Using half white flour or half whole wheat, or a mixture of white, rye, and graham can also open up new possibilities for a recipe.

Following are substitutions that will work for the recipes in this book. These can help you match your own taste preferences or make use of what is on hand.

> 1 package dry yeast (1 tablespoon) = 1 cake compressed
>   yeast (½ ounce)
> 1 teaspoon baking powder = ¼ teaspoon baking soda + ½
>   teaspoon cream of tartar
> 1 cup sugar = 1 cup honey = 1 cup packed brown sugar = 1
>   cup molasses + ½ teaspoon baking soda
> 1 cup all-purpose white flour = 1 cup cornmeal = 1 cup
>   whole wheat flour = 1¼ cups rye flour
> 1 cup buttermilk = 1 cup yogurt = 1 tablespoon lemon juice
>   or vinegar + milk to make 1 cup (let sit 5 minutes)
> 1 cup milk = 1 cup skim milk + 1 tablespoon melted butter
>   = 1 cup water + 4 to 5 tablespoons powdered milk
> 1 cup butter = 1 scant cup bacon fat (omit salt in recipe) = 1
>   scant cup lard + ½ teaspoon salt = 1 cup + 2
>   tablespoons shortening + ½ teaspoon salt

STORING

After sufficient cooling, wrap loaves of quick and batter breads in tinfoil and store in the refrigerator, but use them within a week at the longest. Any bread will keep well in the freezer, for two to three months. Again, wrap each cooled loaf in tinfoil, place in a plastic bag, removing as much air from the bag as possible, secure the end, and freeze.

Rolls and muffins can be packed in plastic bags and placed in the freezer. Thaw them when needed, then bake in a 300° oven for five to ten minutes.

USES FOR STALE BREAD

Bread left out for immediate use can become hard in several days, but there are a number of ways to use it up. Cut it into chunks for dipping into a cheese fondue, soak slices of the bread in a milk-and-egg mixture for French toast, or try any of the following recipes.

CROUTONS

Serve with soups or in salads.

Spread slices of bread with softened butter, or butter mixed with herbs or garlic. Cut into cubes and place on baking sheet. Toast under broiler for several minutes, and turn to brown other side.

BREAD CRUMBS

Use bread crumbs in meatballs and meat loaf, for stuffings, in puddings, and as a topping for a variety of baked dishes. Store them in the freezer in a tightly covered jar.

Dry bread crumbs: Use bread that has been dried out in a low oven or in a toaster. Break into chunks, place in a blender, and whirl at low speed for several seconds. Or place bread between doubled sheets of wax paper or inside a brown paper grocery bag and crush with a rolling pin.

Soft bread crumbs: Crumble bread (with crusts removed) into small pieces, or grate the bread along largest openings of a metal food grater.

BREAD PUDDING

An old-time recipe to use up stale bread.

3 cups milk
⅓ cup sugar
4 tablespoons butter (½ stick)
2 cups coarse bread crumbs

2 eggs
¼ teaspoon salt
1 teaspoon vanilla
½ cup raisins

Preheat oven to 325°. Scald milk, add sugar and butter, and stir until butter melts. Add crumbs and let cool. Beat in eggs, salt, and vanilla. Fold in raisins. Place mixture in buttered 1-quart casserole and bake 1 hour.   *Serves 4-5.*

ORANGE BREAD PUDDING

A change of pace from the traditional recipe.

2½ slices stale bread, broken
   into small pieces
2 cups hot milk
1 large orange
¾ cup granulated sugar

2 eggs, separated
2 teaspoons vanilla
¼ cup powdered sugar
1 teaspoon baking powder
Salt

Preheat oven to 350°. Soak bread in milk for 10 minutes. Add grated rind from orange, granulated sugar, beaten egg yolks, and 1 teaspoon vanilla. Stir well, pour into greased 1-quart casserole, and bake for 45 minutes. Remove from oven. Beat egg whites until stiff with powdered sugar, baking powder, pinch of salt, and remaining teaspoon vanilla. Pour juice of orange over pudding, cover with meringue, and return to oven until lightly browned on top. Serve cool or chilled.   *Serves 4-5.*

EASY CHEESE SOUFFLÉ

Serve with a salad for a complete meal.

1¾ cups milk
4 slices stale, white bread
3 eggs, separated
½ cup cream

Salt, pepper, and nutmeg to
   taste
1 cup grated Swiss cheese (8
   ounces)

Preheat oven to 350°. Scald the milk; cut slices of bread in half, soak in milk, and line bottom of a greased baking dish with them. Beat egg yolks and mix in cream; add milk used for soaking bread, seasonings, and cheese, and stir until blended. Beat egg whites until stiff, fold into mixture, and pour over bread in baking dish. Bake for 25 to 30 minutes, or until knife inserted comes out clean.
                                                   Serves 4-6.

CHEESE MUFF

A variation of the previous recipe.

3 slices stale bread
½ cup softened butter (1 stick)
½ cup sharp cheddar cheese,
   cut into small pieces (4
   ounces)

3 eggs
2 cups milk
Salt and pepper to taste

Preheat oven to 350°. Spread each slice of bread generously with butter; layer in a greased 1½-quart baking dish, sprinkling cheese between the layers. Beat eggs and milk together, season with salt and pepper, and pour over bread. Bake for 45 minutes and serve immediately.

Serves 6.

WELSH RAREBIT

For extra flavor, place a thin slice of fresh tomato on toast before adding sauce.

1 teaspoon dry mustard
½ teaspoon salt
1 teaspoon flour
1 tablespoon water
1 egg

¾ cup milk
2 cups grated cheddar cheese
Dash Tabasco
4 to 5 slices toast

In top of double boiler over hot water mix together mustard, salt, flour, and water to form a smooth paste. Add egg and beat with whisk until smooth. Slowly add milk and stir until blended. Add cheese and stir constantly until melted and smooth. Season with Tabasco. Serve hot on slices of toast.

Serves 2-3.

BAKING EQUIPMENT

You don't need a lot of fancy equipment to make bread, which is part of its appeal. But here are a few suggestions for tools that make the job more satisfying.

Bread Bowl. Crockery bowls hold heat longer than metal or glass bowls, and are better for containing yeast breads as they rise. A good bread bowl should have a capacity of eight to ten quarts, large enough to hold dough for several loaves.

Breadboard. Essential to breadbaking, a good board should be completely smooth and large enough to handle a number of jobs, from rolling out pie crust and kneading bread to shaping rolls and doughnuts. Available in hardwood, marble, and lucite, a breadboard of approximately 18x24 inches is an adequate size.

Electric Mixer. Kneading dough by hand is a satisfying task for people who enjoy making bread. You don't have to have any machines to do the work for you; but a mixer can be a great help to the baker who is in a hurry, and especially useful for kneading stiff, difficult dough such as rye and pumpernickel. The mixer preferred by many professional cooks is the Kitchen-Aid Mixer (K-5A Model), which comes with a dough hook and deep bowl. Use a mixer for initial mixing and blending, then remove dough and give it a final kneading by hand.

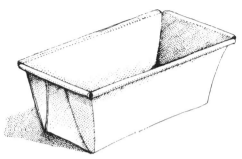

Bread Pan. Loaf pans come in many shapes and sizes. Capacity rather than quarter inches is important in considering what pan to use for a given bread. If bread is to rise until doubled, the pan should be at least as large as the intended height after baking. All baking times in this book are based upon the use of metal pans. Remember as you bake that glass and stoneware hold heat more than metal, so oven temperatures should be lowered by 25° when using them, to prevent crusts from scorching.

Black baker's steel is a durable metal that produces lovely crusts in baked breads. A useful size in this material is 10x5x3½ inches (2¼ quarts). Cheaper aluminum pans give good results as well; a size commonly available and useful for home baking is 8½x4½x3⅛ inches (1½ quarts). Bread can also be baked in Pyrex loaf pans, manufactured in sizes 8½x4½x2½ inches (1½ quarts) and 9x5x3 inches (2 quarts). Bennington Potters makes a stoneware loaf pan, 10x4½x2¼ inches (1½ quarts), that comes in a variety of colors.

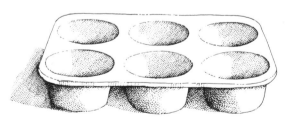

Muffin Pan. Useful for many kinds of rolls, muffins, and popovers, these sectioned pans are available in aluminum, steel, or more expensive cast iron. Pans with 2½- to 3-inch sections are the most versatile. Search in antique shops and flea markets for cast-iron gem pans, which resemble rows of small inverted bread loaves; these make nicely shaped muffins and small, individual batter breads.

Bread Tile. Europeans make crusty bread on heated bricks, a method that is impractical for modern stoves. Unglazed 5½-inch quarry tiles (sold in flooring supply shops) or decorated glazed bread tiles (available in gourmet supply shops) will produce crusty free-form loaves. Four to six tiles will line most ovens. Place them on the middle rack or one rack lower and preheat oven with them in place. Slide bread onto tiles, close the door, and don't reopen for at least 20 minutes. Bake as directed in the recipe.

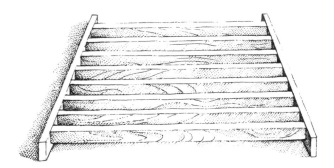

Bread Rack. If you leave most breads in loaf pans to cool, they will become soggy on the bottom. For this reason, and to keep heat in the pan from making the crust tough, breads should be placed on racks to cool. Metal and wooden racks are widely available, and in a variety of sizes.

II.
Yeast Breads

BASIC WHITE BREAD

A good bread for sandwiches.

3 tablespoons sugar
2 tablespoons salt
⅓ cup butter
2 cups milk, scalded
1½ cups cold water

2 packages dry yeast
½ cup warm water
10 to 12 cups white flour
Melted butter

Mix together sugar, salt, butter, and milk. Add cold water. Dissolve
yeast in warm water and add to mixture. Mix in flour, a few cups at
a time, until dough is velvety. Knead until smooth. Place in buttered
bowl, turn to grease top, cover, and let rise for 2 hours. Punch down,
let rise 1 hour more, then shape into 3 loaves. Let rest 10 to 15
minutes. Place each loaf in greased 9½-inch loaf pan. Let rise until
just above the rim of pan. Bake in preheated 425° oven for 10
minutes; then reduce heat to 350° and bake 1 hour. Remove from
pans and brush tops lightly with melted butter to soften crusts.

Makes 3 loaves.

BRICK OVEN WHITE BREAD

*This very light bread contains no fat. It will develop a thick crust if baked
as directed, and should be eaten in a day, since it becomes hard as it sits.*

2 packages dry yeast
½ cup warm water
6 to 7 cups white flour

1½ cups warm water
¼ teaspoon salt

Dissolve yeast in warm water. Beat in 1 cup flour until blended and
shape dough into a ball. Place in ungreased bowl, cover, and let rise
until doubled. Punch down, stir in water and salt, and add 2 cups
flour. Turn mixture out onto floured board and knead in remaining
flour to form a smooth dough. Pat into a round loaf on breadboard,
cover, and let rise until doubled. As dough finishes rising, place
bread tiles (see page 20) in oven and preheat to 400°. Slide loaf onto
hot tiles and bake 50 to 60 minutes. (Do not open door during first
20 minutes.) Cool loaf on its side on bread rack at least 2 hours
before slicing. *Makes 1 loaf.*

OVERNIGHT WHITE BREAD

The long, slow rising required of this bread produces a fine flavor.

2 packages dry yeast
1 cup warm water
6 to 7 cups white flour
2 cups milk
4 tablespoons butter (½ stick)

⅓ cup sugar
1 tablespoon salt
2 eggs
½ teaspoon baking powder

In bread bowl dissolve yeast in warm water. Stir in 2½ cups flour until smooth, cover, and let rise overnight. In the morning, scald milk, add butter, and stir until butter melts. Add sugar and salt. When cool, beat in eggs. Punch down risen dough, and stir in milk and egg mixture. Sift together 2 cups flour and baking powder, and beat into mixture. Add remaining flour, 1 cup at a time, to form a stiff dough. Turn out onto floured board and knead until smooth. Shape into a ball. Place in buttered bowl, turn to grease top, cover, and let rise until doubled. Punch down, divide in half, and place in 2 greased 9-inch loaf pans. Cover and let rise until doubled. Bake in preheated 300° oven 40 to 50 minutes. *Makes 2 loaves.*

WHITE NUT BREAD

A light yet moist bread, wonderful toasted. The nuts "disappear" in baking.

2 packages dry yeast
½ cup warm water
2 cups milk
4 tablespoons butter (½ stick)

2 teaspoons salt
⅓ cup brown sugar
7 cups white flour
½ cup finely chopped walnuts

Dissolve yeast in warm water and set aside. Scald milk, add butter, and stir until butter melts. Add salt and brown sugar and stir until sugar is dissolved. Pour mixture into bread bowl, add yeast, and stir until blended. Beat in flour, 1 cup at a time, to form a stiff dough. Turn out onto floured board and knead in nuts until dough is smooth. Shape into a ball. Place in buttered bowl, turn to grease top, cover, and let rise until doubled. Punch down, divide in half, and place in 2 greased 8-inch loaf pans. Cover and let rise until doubled. Bake in preheated 350° oven 30 to 40 minutes. *Makes 2 loaves.*

WHITE RICE BREAD

White rice gives this the taste and texture of an old-fashioned white bread. Use whole wheat flour and brown rice for a heavier loaf.

2 packages dry yeast
¼ cup warm water
2 teaspoons sugar
1 teaspoon salt

4 cups white flour
1 cup cooked rice (white rice
　should be cooked in milk)
1¾ cups milk, warmed

Dissolve yeast in warm water and set aside. Mix together sugar, salt, and flour. Mash cooked rice. In large bowl, using your hands, rub rice into flour. Stir in yeast and milk. Turn out onto floured board and knead until smooth. Place in buttered bowl, turn to grease top, cover, and let rise until doubled. Punch down, halve, and place in 2 greased 8½-inch loaf pans. Cover and let rise again. Bake at 350° until brown, 45 to 55 minutes. *Makes 2 loaves.*

QUICK FRENCH BREAD

Serve warm with lots of butter.

1 package dry yeast
1½ cups warm water
2 tablespoons sugar
½ teaspoon salt

1 tablespoon melted butter
4 to 5 cups white flour
Melted butter

Dissolve yeast in ½ cup warm water and set aside. In bread bowl stir together remaining water, sugar, and salt. Add yeast and butter and stir until blended. Beat in flour, 1 cup at a time, to form a soft dough. Turn out onto floured board. Knead 1 minute, let sit 10 minutes, knead again, and let sit 10 minutes. Divide dough in half and roll each out into a rectangle about 8x12 inches. Starting at the long end, roll up tightly. Place seam-side down on ungreased baking sheet, slash top every 2 inches with a sharp knife, cover, and let rise until doubled. Bake in preheated 400° oven 30 to 40 minutes. Place on racks to cool and brush tops with melted butter. *Makes 2 loaves.*

For Garlic Bread: Cut a loaf of French bread into 1- to 1½-inch slices, leaving each piece attached to the loaf at the base. Cream 1 stick of softened butter, 2 minced cloves of garlic, and, if desired, 1 tablespoon minced chervil or parsley. Season to taste with salt and pepper. Spread each slice with mixture, wrap loaf in tinfoil, and bake 20 minutes in preheated 350° oven.

TANGY BREAD STICKS

A savory accompaniment to appetizers, soups, or salads.

4 cups flour
3 tablespoons sugar
2 teaspoons salt
1 package dry yeast
1 cup water
1 tablespoon butter

1 tablespoon caraway seed
½ teaspoon Tabasco
1 teaspoon dry oregano
Melted butter
Coarse salt

Combine 1 cup flour, sugar, salt, and yeast in large bowl. In saucepan heat water, add butter, and stir until melted. Add cooled wet ingredients to dry in bowl and beat 2 minutes. Add ½ cup flour, caraway seed, Tabasco, and oregano. Beat 2 minutes longer. Add remaining flour, ½ cup at a time, to form a soft dough. Turn out onto floured board and knead until smooth. Place in buttered bowl and turn to grease top. Cover and let rise until doubled. Punch down. Divide dough into 24 equal pieces. Roll each piece into a stick about 8 inches long. Place on greased baking sheets. Cover and let rise until doubled. Brush with melted butter and sprinkle with coarse salt. Bake in preheated 400° oven 15 to 20 minutes.   *Makes 2 dozen.*

PRETZELS

Use a mixer for best results.

2 packages dry yeast
2 cups warm water
¼ cup sugar
2 teaspoons salt
6 to 7 cups flour

3 tablespoons melted butter
2 eggs
1 egg yolk, beaten
2 tablespoons milk
Coarse salt

Dissolve yeast in ½ cup warm water and set aside. Sift together sugar, salt, and 5 cups flour. Combine yeast, remaining water, butter, and 2 eggs in mixing bowl and blend. Beat in flour mixture, 1 cup at a time, to make a stiff dough, adding all or a portion of the remaining flour if necessary. Cover with plastic wrap and refrigerate overnight. Next day, divide chilled dough in half, roll each out into a rope, and cut each into 12 equal pieces. Roll each piece between your palms until pencil thin. Twist into desired shapes and pinch ends together, or keep as straight rods. Combine egg yolk and milk, and brush on each piece. Sprinkle with coarse salt. Place on greased baking sheet, cover, and let rise for 45 minutes. Bake in preheated 400° oven 15 minutes.   *Makes 2 dozen.*

ANADAMA BREAD

Numerous legends surround the title of this bread. A popular one refers to a woman named Anna, who was cursed by her husband for being lazy.

1 package dry yeast	2 tablespoons butter
2 cups warm water	or bacon fat
1 teaspoon salt	4 to 5 cups flour
½ cup cornmeal	Melted butter
½ cup molasses	

Dissolve yeast in ¼ cup warm water and set aside. Pour remaining water into large saucepan, add salt, and bring to a boil. Stir in cornmeal, bring to a boil, remove from heat, and add molasses and butter. Stir until butter melts and mixture cools. Pour into bread bowl. Add yeast and beat in flour, 1 cup at a time, to form a stiff dough. Turn out onto floured board and knead until smooth. Shape into a ball. Place in buttered bowl, turn to grease top, cover, and let rise until doubled. Punch down, knead, divide in half, and place in 2 greased 9-inch loaf pans. Cover and let rise until doubled. Bake in preheated 375° oven 40 to 50 minutes or until brown. Remove loaves from pans and brush with melted butter. *Makes 2 loaves.*

RISEN CORN BREAD

A light corn bread to serve with soups and stews, or as the under "biscuit" for creamed entrées.

1 package dry yeast	2 tablespoons sugar
¼ cup warm water	2 eggs, beaten
1 cup milk	2 cups flour
2 tablespoons butter	1 teaspoon salt
1 cup cornmeal	

Dissolve yeast in warm water and set aside. Scald milk and stir in butter until melted. Pour into bread bowl. Add cornmeal and sugar, and stir until smooth. Mix in eggs and yeast. Sift together flour and salt, and beat into wet ingredients to form a stiff dough. Place bowl in pan of hot water, cover, and let rise until doubled. (Renew hot water as necessary.) Punch down, place in greased 9-inch square pan, and let rise until doubled. Bake in preheated 375° oven 20 to 30 minutes. *Serves 8-10.*

CARROT BREAD

The carrot adds more color than flavor to this bread, which is especially good toasted.

1 package dry yeast
½ cup warm orange juice
1 tablespoon honey
2 tablespoons melted butter

½ teaspoon salt
1 cup grated carrots
3 to 4 cups flour

Combine yeast and warm orange juice in bread bowl and set aside. When bubbly, stir in honey, butter, salt, and carrots. Beat in flour, 1 cup at a time, to form a soft dough. Place in greased 9-inch loaf pan. Cover and let rise until doubled. Bake in preheated 200° oven 20 minutes; increase heat to 300° and bake 35 minutes longer.

Makes 1 loaf.

PUMPKIN BREAD

For a subtle difference substitute Hubbard, acorn, or butternut squash.

2 packages dry yeast
¼ cup warm water
1 cup pumpkin, canned, or
    cooked and mashed
2 tablespoons sugar

1 teaspoon salt
1½ cups milk
1 tablespoon butter
3 to 4 cups flour

Dissolve yeast in warm water. Add pumpkin, sugar, and salt. Scald milk, add butter, and stir until melted. When cool, blend with pumpkin mixture. Add flour, 1 cup at a time, to form a stiff dough. Turn out onto floured board and knead until smooth. Place in buttered bowl, turn to grease top, cover, and let rise until doubled. Punch down, knead, divide in half, and place in 2 greased 8-inch loaf pans. Cover and let rise until doubled. Bake in preheated 350° oven 40 to 50 minutes.

Makes 2 loaves.

SWEET POTATO BREAD

Crusty, lovely-looking bread with a nut-like flavor.

7 to 7½ cups white flour
1½ cups whole wheat flour
1 tablespoon sugar
1½ teaspoons salt
2 packages dry yeast
4 tablespoons melted butter
 (½ stick)

2 cups very warm water
1½ cups cooked, mashed
 sweet potatoes
¼ cup toasted sesame seed
1 egg white
1 tablespoon water

Mix 5½ cups white flour with all the whole wheat flour. Pour 2⅓ cups of this flour mixture into a bowl and add sugar, salt, and yeast. Mix in butter and gradually stir in 2 cups water. Beat 2 minutes with electric mixer at medium speed and scrape bowl from time to time. Add sweet potatoes and ½ cup of flour mixture, and beat at high speed for 2 minutes. Mix in remaining flour mixture, ½ cup at a time, and enough additional white flour to make a soft dough. Turn out onto floured board and knead until smooth. Place in buttered bowl, turn to grease top, cover, and let rise until doubled, about 1 hour. Punch down and knead in 3 tablespoons sesame seed. Divide dough in half, place in 2 greased 9-inch loaf pans, cover, and let rise until doubled. Mix egg white with 1 tablespoon water and brush over tops of loaves. Sprinkle with remaining sesame seed and bake in preheated 375° oven for 35 to 40 minutes, or until done.

Makes 2 loaves.

CHEESE BREAD I

A chewy bread with a delightful fragrance.

4 to 4½ cups flour
¼ cup sugar
1 teaspoon salt
2 packages dry yeast
½ cup water

1 cup milk
4 tablespoons butter (½ stick)
3½ cups grated cheese
 (preferably cheddar)

Combine 2 cups flour, sugar, salt, and yeast. In saucepan heat water, milk, and butter until butter melts. Cool, add to dry ingredients, and beat with mixer 2 minutes at medium speed. Add ½ cup flour. Beat 2 minutes longer. Add cheese and remaining flour, ½ cup at a time, to make a smooth dough. Turn out onto floured board and knead until smooth. Shape into a ball. Place in buttered bowl, turn to grease top, cover, and let rise until doubled. Punch down, divide in half, and place in 2 greased 8-inch loaf pans. Cover and let rise until doubled. Bake in preheated 375° oven 30 minutes. *Makes 2 loaves.*

CHEESE BREAD II

Complements chili and Italian dishes.

5 to 6 cups white flour
2 packages dry yeast
1 tablespoon sugar
1 teaspoon salt
1½ teaspoons dry mustard
Dash of Tabasco
2 cups milk

1 cup cubed cheddar cheese
  (8 ounces)
2 tablespoons butter
1½ tablespoons
  Worcestershire sauce
Melted butter

In large bowl combine 2 cups flour, yeast, sugar, salt, and mustard. In saucepan heat Tabasco and milk; stir in cheese and butter, and cook over low heat until melted. Cool, add dry ingredients, and beat 3 minutes. Add Worcestershire and remaining flour, ½ cup at a time, to form a smooth dough. Turn onto floured board and knead until smooth, 6 to 8 minutes. Place in buttered bowl, turn to grease top, and cover. Let rise until doubled, about 1 hour. Punch down and divide into halves. Roll into two 5x11-inch rectangles. Cut each into 3 long strips, join strips at one end, and braid. Place braids in 2 greased 8-inch loaf pans. Brush with melted butter and let rise in warm place until doubled, about 1 hour. Bake at 350° for 45 to 55 minutes. *Makes 2 loaves.*

CHEESE BREAD III

Experiment with a wide variety of cheeses to discover your favorite flavors.

1 package dry yeast
¼ cup warm water
1½ cups milk
2 tablespoons butter
Dash of Tabasco

1 tablespoon sugar
6 to 7 cups flour
1 cup grated cheese (cheddar,
  Parmesan, Gouda, etc.)

Dissolve yeast in warm water and set aside. Scald milk, add butter, Tabasco, and sugar, and stir until butter melts. When cool, combine with yeast in bread bowl. Alternately beat in flour, 1 cup at a time, and cheese, ¼ cup at a time, to form a stiff dough. Turn out onto floured board and knead until smooth. Shape into a ball. Place in buttered bowl, turn to grease top, cover, and let rise until doubled. Punch down, knead, divide in half, and place in 2 greased 9-inch loaf pans. Cover and let rise until doubled. Bake in preheated 400° oven 35 to 45 minutes. *Makes 2 loaves.*

BASIL BREAD

To change the taste entirely, try other dry herbs such as dill, marjoram, or thyme, and a mixture of white, whole wheat, and rye flours.

2 packages dry yeast	¼ cup sugar
½ cup warm water	2 teaspoons salt
½ cup butter (1 stick)	1½ cups milk
2 teaspoons dry basil	7 to 8 cups flour

Dissolve yeast in warm water and set aside. Melt butter in saucepan, add basil, sugar, and salt, and stir until sugar dissolves. Add milk and heat until warm. Pour mixture into bread bowl and add yeast. Beat in flour, 1 cup at a time, to form a stiff dough. Turn out onto floured board and knead until smooth. Shape into a ball. Place in buttered bowl, turn to grease top, cover, and let rise until doubled. Punch down, divide between 2 greased 9-inch loaf pans, cover, and let rise until doubled. Bake in preheated 375° oven 40 to 50 minutes.

Makes 2 loaves.

CHIVE BREAD

A light-textured bread that goes well with beef.

1 package dry yeast	3 tablespoons melted butter
½ cup warm water	½ cup chopped chives
1 egg, beaten	3 cups flour (or more)
½ teaspoon salt	

Dissolve yeast in warm water. Stir in egg, salt, butter, and chives. Beat in flour, 1 cup at a time, to form a stiff dough. Turn out onto floured board and knead until smooth and elastic. Shape into a ball. Place in buttered bowl, turn to grease top, cover, and let rise until doubled. Punch down, place in greased 9-inch loaf pan, cover, and let rise until doubled. Bake in preheated 350° oven for 50 minutes.

Makes 1 loaf.

DILL BREAD

A lovely luncheon bread.

1 package dry yeast
¼ cup warm water
2 tablespoons sugar
1 tablespoon butter
½ teaspoon salt
1 egg, beaten
1 cup yogurt
2 tablespoons finely minced
  onion

½ teaspoon baking soda
2 tablespoons chopped fresh
  dill weed, or 1 tablespoon
  dry
2 cups flour (white, whole
  wheat, or combination)
Melted butter
Coarse salt

Dissolve yeast in warm water. Add all but last two ingredients and mix well. Cover and let rise until doubled. Stir down. Divide between 2 greased 7-inch loaf pans. Bake in preheated 350° oven 30 minutes. Remove from oven, turn out on racks, brush tops with melted butter, and sprinkle with coarse salt.   *Makes 2 loaves.*

DILLY CASSEROLE BREAD

Cut in wedges or turn out of the dish and cut across the loaf into long slices.

1 package dry yeast
¼ cup warm water
1 cup creamed cottage cheese
2 tablespoons sugar
1 tablespoon melted butter
1 tablespoon dried minced
  onion

1 egg, beaten
2 teaspoons dill seed
1 teaspoon salt
¼ teaspoon baking soda
2 to 2½ cups flour
Melted butter
Salt

Soak yeast in warm water. Heat cottage cheese until warm; stir in sugar, butter, onion, egg, dill seed, salt, soda, and yeast mixture. Gradually add flour to make a stiff dough, mixing well. Cover and let rise until doubled. Punch down, turn into well-greased 8-inch round casserole dish (1½-quart capacity), and let rise again until doubled. Bake in preheated 350° oven for 40 to 50 minutes. Remove to rack, brush top with butter, and sprinkle with salt.

Makes 1 loaf.

HERB BREAD

Use this fine, soft-textured loaf for sandwiches.

2 packages dry yeast
¼ cup warm water
¼ cup sugar
1 small onion, minced
1 teaspoon salt
1 tablespoon chopped fresh
    marjoram or thyme
1 tablespoon chopped fresh
    parsley

2 eggs
2 cups warm milk
4 tablespoons melted butter
    (½ stick)
7 to 8 cups flour (white, whole
    wheat, or combination)

Dissolve yeast in warm water. Add remaining ingredients except flour and mix thoroughly. Add flour, ½ cup at a time, to form a stiff dough. Turn out onto floured board and knead until smooth, 6 to 8 minutes. Shape into a ball. Place in buttered bowl, turn to grease top, cover, and let rise until doubled. Punch down and divide in half. Place in 2 greased 8½-inch loaf pans, cover, and let rise until doubled. Bake in preheated 425° oven 25 to 35 minutes.

Makes 2 loaves.

ROLLED HERB BREAD

Roll up tightly, to decrease spaces between filling and dough in the spiraled slices.

2 packages dry yeast
½ cup warm water
1½ cups milk
4 tablespoons butter (½ stick)
1 tablespoon sugar
2 teaspoons salt
6 to 7 cups flour
2 tablespoons butter
2½ cups finely chopped fresh
    chervil or parsley

1 cup finely chopped shallots
1 cup finely chopped scallions
2 cloves garlic, minced
2 eggs, beaten
1 teaspoon salt
1 egg
1 tablespoon milk
Melted butter

Dissolve yeast in warm water and set aside. Scald 1½ cups milk, add 4 tablespoons butter, the sugar, and 2 teaspoons salt; stir until butter melts. Pour milk mixture into bread bowl, and when cool, add yeast and beat in flour, 1 cup at a time, to form a stiff dough. Turn out onto floured board and knead until smooth. Shape into a ball. Place in buttered bowl, turn to grease top, cover, and let rise until doubled. As dough rises, melt 2 tablespoons butter in saucepan and sauté chervil, shallots, scallions, and garlic until soft. Cool and beat in 2 eggs and 1 teaspoon salt. Set aside.

Punch down risen dough, turn onto lightly floured board, and cut into 2 equal pieces. Roll out each into a rectangle ¼ inch thick and about 8 inches wide. Beat together 1 egg and 1 tablespoon milk, and brush onto both pieces of dough. Spread herb filling over dough, leaving about 1½ inches clear all around the edges. Roll up tightly, starting at 1 short end. Pinch edges together and place seam-side down in 2 greased 9-inch loaf pans. Cover and let rise until doubled. Brush tops with melted butter and bake in preheated 400° oven 50 to 60 minutes. *Makes 2 loaves.*

SOUR CREAM HERB BREAD

Use fresh herbs if available for the best flavor.

2 packages dry yeast
½ cup warm water
1 cup sour cream or yogurt
4 tablespoons melted butter
   (½ stick)
1 teaspoon salt
¼ cup sugar
1 tablespoon finely chopped
   oregano or thyme leaves
2 eggs
4 to 5 cups flour

Dissolve yeast in warm water and set aside. Blend together sour cream, butter, salt, sugar, herb leaves, and eggs. Add yeast. Beat in flour, 1 cup at a time, to form a soft dough. Cover and let rise until doubled. Punch down, turn out onto floured board, and knead until smooth. Divide and place in 2 greased 9-inch loaf pans. Cover and let rise until doubled. Bake in preheated 375° oven 30 to 40 minutes. *Makes 2 loaves.*

HERB AND ONION BREAD

Serve this hearty bread with soups or cheese.

2 packages dry yeast
¼ cup warm water
2 cups milk
2 tablespoons butter
3 cups whole wheat flour
3 cups white flour

1 teaspoon salt
1 onion, minced
1½ cups finely chopped
    parsley, thyme,
    or other herb

Dissolve yeast in warm water. Scald milk and stir in butter until melted. Combine flours and salt, add yeast and cooled milk mixture. Blend well. Turn out onto floured board and knead in onion and herbs, working to distribute them evenly through the dough. Divide dough in half and place in 2 greased 8-inch loaf pans. Cover and let rise until doubled. Bake in preheated 375° oven 50 to 60 minutes.

Makes 2 loaves.

ROLLED ONION BREAD

A flavorful loaf for brunch or lunch.

2 packages dry yeast
½ cup warm water
3 cups milk
4 tablespoons butter (½ stick)
⅓ cup sugar
7 to 8 cups flour
2 eggs, beaten

8 cardamom seeds, crushed
2 tablespoons butter
4 medium onions, peeled and
    minced
Salt and pepper to taste
2 tablespoons cold black coffee

Dissolve yeast in warm water and set aside. Scald milk, add 4 tablespoons butter and the sugar, and stir until butter melts. Cool. In bread bowl combine yeast and milk mixtures. Beat in 4 cups flour, 1 cup at a time, then eggs, cardamom seeds, and remaining flour to form a stiff dough. Turn out onto floured board and knead until smooth. Shape into a ball. Place in buttered bowl, turn to grease top, cover, and let rise until doubled. As dough rises, melt 2 tablespoons butter in skillet and sauté onions until soft. Set aside.

Punch down risen dough, turn out onto floured board, and knead briefly. Roll out into rectangle ½ inch thick. Cut in half width-wise. Spread 1 piece with sautéed onion and butter mixture. Season with salt and pepper. Cover with other half of dough, pinch edges together, and roll up tightly. Place in greased 9-inch loaf pan, cover, and let rise until doubled. Brush with cold coffee and bake in preheated 325° oven 25 to 35 minutes, or until brown.　*Makes 1 loaf.*

SALT-RISING BREAD

When successfully made, this bread has a delicious taste and unusual texture; but it is one of the most temperamental of all risen breads. The starter mixture must foam as instructions indicate, or recipe will not work. Starter must be kept warm (around 100°) during its fermentation period. Keep in electric oven on low heat, or put your Yankee ingenuity to work. Cooks of old wrapped mixture in heavy quilts, and renewed the boiling water as needed.

THE STARTER

2 small potatoes, peeled and
   thinly sliced
3 tablespoons cornmeal

2 tablespoons sugar
1 teaspoon salt
2 cups boiling water

Combine above ingredients and pour into warm 2-quart jar. Cover with lid, place jar in deep kettle or bowl, and add boiling water so jar is almost immersed, leaving cap out of water. Cover with a heavy towel and keep warm for 10 to 20 hours, until foam develops on top to a depth of at least ½ inch. (If foam does not develop, discard and start again.) When top is foamy, strain liquid into a bowl, pressing potatoes gently with a wooden spoon to extract as much liquid as possible. Discard potatoes.

THE BREAD

½ cup milk
2 tablespoons butter
1½ teaspoons salt
Starter liquid

½ teaspoon baking soda
5 to 6 cups flour
Melted butter

Heat milk, add butter and salt, and stir until butter melts. When lukewarm, combine in bowl with starter liquid and soda. Beat in 4 cups flour, 1 cup at a time, to form a soft dough. Turn out onto floured board and knead in 1 to 2 cups more flour to form a soft, smooth dough. Halve and place in 2 greased 8-inch loaf pans. Cover and let rise until doubled (allow as long as 6 hours for this rising). Brush tops with melted butter and bake in preheated 375° oven 40 to 50 minutes. *Makes 2 loaves.*

SOURDOUGH STARTER I

Begin making the starter several days before you want to bake sourdough bread.

2 cups milk
2 cups flour (any kind)

Measure milk into wide-mouth canning jar. Let stand, uncovered, 24 hours. (Or, cover with a piece of cheesecloth and attach with just the canning ring.) Stir in flour and place in draft-free area (65° to 85°) for 2 to 3 days. When milk sours and mixture shows signs of activity, starter is ready to use in breadmaking. Either use now or remove cheesecloth and store, covered, in refrigerator. Each time you pour some starter out, replace it with equal amounts of milk and flour. Use some of the starter every 4 to 5 days.

SOURDOUGH STARTER II

Adding yeast will hasten the souring process.

2 cups warm beer
1 teaspoon sugar
1 teaspoon salt
1 teaspoon dry yeast
  (optional)
1 cup flour

Combine all ingredients in a jar, stir until blended, and let sit at room temperature until fermented (about 2 days). If yeast is used, mixture is ready when it shows signs of bubbling and begins to grow.

SOURDOUGH BREAD

A moist, fragrant bread, heavenly toasted and smothered with butter.

2 packages dry yeast
1½ cups warm water
4 to 5 cups flour
3 teaspoons sugar
1 teaspoon salt
1 teaspoon baking soda
1 cup sourdough starter

Dissolve yeast in ½ cup warm water and set aside. Sift together 4 cups flour, sugar, salt, and soda. Pour remaining 1 cup warm water into yeast and stir in starter. Gradually add dry ingredients, 1 cup at a time, stirring to form a stiff dough. (Add more flour as necessary.) Turn out onto floured board and knead until smooth. Place in buttered bowl, turn to grease top, cover, and let rise until doubled. Punch down, knead several minutes, and shape into round loaf. Place on greased baking sheet, cover, and let rise until doubled. Bake in preheated 400° oven 35 to 45 minutes or until brown.

Makes 1 loaf.

SOURDOUGH HERB BREAD

Use either of the sourdough starters for this aromatic bread.

1 cup sourdough starter
1½ cups warm water
1 teaspoon salt
2 teaspoons sugar
3 tablespoons melted butter

1 teaspoon dried sage
1 teaspoon dried thyme
1 teaspoon dried basil
3 to 4 cups flour

Mix together starter, water, salt, sugar, and butter. Sift together herbs and 3 cups flour. Work into starter mixture, beating in additional flour as needed to form a soft dough. Shape into a ball. Place in greased bowl, turn to grease top, cover, and let rise until doubled. Punch down, turn out onto floured board, and knead until smooth. Place in greased 9-inch loaf pan. Cover and let rise until doubled. Bake in preheated 375° oven 40 to 50 minutes.

Makes 1 loaf.

BEER BREAD

Tastes terrific.

½ cup warm water
2 packages dry yeast
½ cup sugar
2 teaspoons salt

1 can (12 ounces) warm beer
4 tablespoons melted butter
  (½ stick)
6 to 7 cups flour

Combine water, yeast, sugar, salt, beer, and butter. Beat in flour, 1 cup at a time, to form a stiff dough. Knead on floured board until smooth and elastic. Shape into a ball, place in buttered bowl, and turn to grease top. Cover and let rise until doubled. Punch down, halve, and place in 2 greased 9-inch pans. Cover and let rise again until doubled. Bake in preheated 375° oven 25 to 30 minutes.

Makes 2 loaves.

PUMPERNICKEL BREAD

Cut this chewy, dark bread into thin slices and serve with cold meat and cheese.

2 packages dry yeast
½ cup warm water
2 cups hot water
2 teaspoons salt
4 tablespoons molasses

1 cup mashed potatoes
6½ cups rye flour
2 to 3 cups whole wheat flour
Cornmeal

Dissolve yeast in warm water and set aside. Combine hot water, salt, molasses, and potatoes, and beat until smooth. Cool. Stir in yeast and blend in flours, 1 cup at a time, to form a stiff dough. Turn out onto floured board and knead well. Place in buttered bowl, turn to grease top, cover, and let rise 1 to 2 hours, until doubled. Punch down, knead vigorously, and let rise 30 minutes. Punch down again, knead lightly, and shape into 2 round loaves. Place on greased baking sheet, or put into 2 round 8- or 9-inch greased pans. Cover and let rise until doubled. Brush tops with water and sprinkle generously with cornmeal. Bake in preheated 375° oven 1 to 1¼ hours. *Makes 2 loaves.*

RYE BREAD

A mild-flavored loaf.

3 packages dry yeast
½ cup warm water
1½ cups milk
5 tablespoons butter
3 tablespoons dark molasses
3 cups rye flour
1 cup whole wheat flour

1 cup white flour
¼ cup wheat germ
1 teaspoon salt
3 tablespoons sour cream
2 tablespoons caraway seed
  (optional)
Milk

Dissolve yeast in warm water. Scald milk, add butter and molasses, and stir until butter melts. Combine flours, wheat germ, and salt in bread bowl; stir in cooled milk mixture, yeast, and sour cream. Turn out onto floured board and knead (adding caraway if used), working until dough is smooth and elastic. Shape into a ball. Place in buttered bowl, turn to grease top, cover, and let rise until doubled. Punch down and place in 2 greased 9-inch loaf pans. Cover and let rise until doubled. Brush tops with milk and bake in preheated 425° oven 15 minutes. Reduce heat to 325° and bake 30 minutes longer. *Makes 2 loaves.*

ONION RYE BREAD

Serve with roast pork and a fruit salad.

2 packages dry yeast
½ cup warm water
2½ cups milk
⅓ cup sugar
1 tablespoon salt
4 tablespoons butter (½ stick)

4 tablespoons caraway seed
2 medium onions, peeled and
    chopped
6 cups white flour
2 to 3 cups rye flour
Milk

Dissolve yeast in warm water and set aside. Scald milk, add sugar, salt, and butter, and stir until butter melts. Cool. In bread bowl combine yeast and milk mixtures. Add caraway seed and onions, and beat in white flour, 1 cup at a time. Turn out onto floured board and knead in rye flour to form a stiff dough. Shape into a ball. Place in buttered bowl, turn to grease top, cover, and let rise until doubled. Punch down and knead briefly. Let rise again until doubled. Halve dough and place in 2 greased 9-inch or 3 greased 8-inch loaf pans. Brush tops with milk. Cover and let rise until doubled. Bake in preheated 350° oven 50 to 60 minutes.

Makes 2-3 loaves.

RYE RAISIN BREAD

A wonderful combination of fruit and flours.

2 packages dry yeast
½ cup warm water
2 cups milk
⅓ cup sugar
4 tablespoons melted butter
    (½ stick)
1½ cups raisins

Rind of 1 large orange, grated
2 teaspoons salt
4 cups rye flour
2 to 3 cups white flour
Cornmeal
Cold milk

Dissolve yeast in warm water and set aside. Scald milk, add sugar and butter, and stir until butter melts. Add raisins and let sit 10 minutes. In bread bowl combine yeast and milk mixtures. Add orange rind and beat in salt and rye flour to form a sticky dough. Turn out onto floured board and knead in white flour until smooth. (Don't skimp on the kneading time; work dough about 20 minutes.) Shape into a ball. Place in buttered bowl, turn to grease top, cover, and let rise until doubled. Punch down, turn out onto floured board, knead again, and divide in half. Grease a large baking sheet and sprinkle with cornmeal. Shape dough into 2 round loaves and place on baking sheet. Slash tops with sharp knife, cover, and let rise until doubled. Brush with cold milk and bake in preheated 375° oven 50 to 60 minutes.

Makes 2 loaves.

WHOLE WHEAT BREAD I

Smells as great as it tastes.

2 packages dry yeast
¼ cup warm water
1½ cups milk
1 tablespoon butter

1 teaspoon salt
½ cup molasses
5 to 6 cups whole wheat flour

Dissolve yeast in warm water and set aside. Scald milk, remove from heat, and stir in butter until melted. Add salt and molasses, and blend. Cool and stir in yeast. Beat in flour, 1 cup at a time, to form a stiff dough. Turn out onto floured board and knead until smooth. Place in buttered bowl, turn to grease top, cover, and let rise until doubled. Punch down, knead, and place in 1 greased 9-inch or 2 greased 8-inch loaf pans. Cover and let rise until doubled. Bake in preheated 300° oven 1 to 1½ hours.   *Makes 1-2 loaves.*

WHOLE WHEAT BREAD II

A variation of the previous recipe.

2 cups milk
3 tablespoons oil
1 teaspoon salt
½ cup honey

2 packages dry yeast
⅓ cup warm water
5½ cups whole wheat flour

Pour milk into saucepan, heat to simmer, add oil, salt, and honey, and stir. Cool to lukewarm. Dissolve yeast in warm water and add to cooled milk mixture. Add 3 cups flour, mix well; add 2 cups more flour and mix well. Knead until smooth and elastic, adding more flour as necessary. Place in buttered bowl, turn to coat, cover, and let rise for 1 hour, or until doubled. Punch down, cover and let rise again until doubled. Punch down, place in 2 greased 8½-inch loaf pans, and let rise again until doubled. Bake at 375° for about 45 minutes.   *Makes 2 loaves.*

HONEY WHOLE WHEAT BREAD

For a heavier bread, use only whole wheat flour.

1½ cups water
1 cup cottage cheese
½ cup honey
4 tablespoons butter (½ stick)
5½ to 6 cups white flour

1 cup whole wheat flour
3 teaspoons salt
2 packages dry yeast
1 egg

Heat first 4 ingredients until very warm (about 120°). Pour into large bowl, add 2 cups white flour and remaining ingredients, and beat at medium speed with electric mixer for 2 minutes. Stirring by hand, add enough white flour, 1 cup at a time, to make a stiff dough. Knead dough on floured board until smooth and elastic. Shape into a ball, place in buttered bowl, turn to grease top, cover, and let rise until doubled. Punch down, divide in half, and place in 2 greased 9-inch loaf pans. Cover and let rise until doubled. Bake in preheated 350° oven for 40 to 50 minutes, or until loaves sound hollow when tapped on bottom. *Makes 2 loaves.*

WINDY HILL WHOLE WHEAT BREAD

Full of goodness.

2½ cups milk
¼ cup oil or butter
¼ cup molasses
3 cups whole wheat flour
¼ cup brown sugar
1 tablespoon salt
2 packages dry yeast

3 tablespoons wheat germ (or Ralston or Roman Meal cereal)
3 tablespoons sunflower seed
2 tablespoons sesame seed
1 egg
3 cups white flour

In saucepan scald milk, add oil and molasses, and set aside to cool. Combine 2 cups whole wheat flour, brown sugar, salt, yeast, wheat germ, and seeds. Add warm milk mixture and egg, and beat until smooth. Beat in remaining 1 cup whole wheat flour and the white flour, 1 cup at a time, to form a stiff dough. Turn out onto floured board and knead until smooth. Shape into a ball. Place in buttered bowl, turn to grease top, cover, and let rise until doubled. Punch down and place in 2 greased 9-inch or 3 greased 7½-inch loaf pans. Cover and let rise until doubled. Bake in preheated 350° oven 30 to 40 minutes. *Makes 2-3 loaves.*

For Whole Wheat Raisin Bread: Knead in ½ cup raisins that have soaked for 1 hour in 1 teaspoon rum plus hot water to cover.

BULGUR WHEAT BREAD

Take this bread along on a picnic and serve with wine and cheese.

1 package dry yeast
½ cup warm water
¼ cup bulgur wheat
¾ cup water
1 cup milk

3 tablespoons butter
1 teaspoon salt
2 tablespoons sugar
4 to 5 cups flour

Dissolve yeast in ½ cup warm water and set aside. Combine bulgur and ¾ cup water in small saucepan and simmer (do not boil) 15 minutes, or until bulgur is tender. Do not drain. Set aside to cool. Scald milk, add butter, remove from heat, and stir until butter is melted. Stir in salt and sugar. Combine cooled milk mixture with yeast in bread bowl. Add bulgur. Beat in flour, 1 cup at a time, to form a soft dough. Turn out onto floured board and knead until smooth. Place dough in buttered bowl, turn to grease top, cover, and let rise until doubled. Punch down and knead again. Divide in half and place in 2 greased 8½-inch loaf pans. Cover and let rise until doubled. Bake in preheated 400° oven 30 to 40 minutes.

Makes 2 loaves.

SHREDDED WHEAT BREAD

Tastes like oatmeal bread.

1 cup water
1 cup milk
⅓ cup sugar
1 package dry yeast
2 large Shredded Wheat
    biscuits, crumbled

2 tablespoons molasses
3 tablespoons melted butter
¼ teaspoon salt
4 cups flour
Melted butter

Scald milk and add water and sugar, stirring until sugar dissolves. Cool slightly. Measure ½ cup liquid into bread bowl, add yeast, and stir until dissolved. Add remaining liquid, Shredded Wheat, molasses, butter, and salt, and mix well. Beat in flour to form a stiff dough. Cover and let rise until doubled. Punch down, turn out onto floured board, and knead several minutes. Halve dough, place in 2 greased 9-inch loaf pans, cover, and let rise until doubled. Bake in preheated 375° oven 25 to 35 minutes. Brush baked loaves with melted butter.

Makes 2 loaves.

OATMEAL BREAD I

Moist, delicious, and nutritious.

2 packages dry yeast
2 cups warm water
1 cup quick oats
2 tablespoons butter

⅔ cup molasses
2 eggs
5 to 6 cups flour

Dissolve yeast in ¼ cup warm water. Bring remaining water to a
boil, add oats, butter, and molasses, and cook over low heat 5
minutes. Remove from heat and cool. Pour into bread bowl, add
yeast, and stir until blended. Add eggs and beat in flour, 1 cup at a
time, to form a soft dough. Cover and let rise until doubled. Punch
down, turn onto floured board, and knead gently for 1 minute.
Divide in half and place in 2 greased 9-inch loaf pans. Cover and let
rise until doubled. Bake in preheated 375° oven 50 to 60 minutes.

Makes 2 loaves.

OATMEAL BREAD II

*Especially good if made with a half-and-half mixture of white and whole
wheat flours.*

1 cup rolled oats
2 cups boiling water
2 packages dry yeast
⅓ cup lukewarm water

1 tablespoon salt
½ cup honey
2 tablespoons melted butter
4 to 5 cups flour

Put oats in large bread bowl and pour in boiling water. Stir and set
aside for 30 minutes. Soak yeast in warm water. Add salt, honey,
and butter to oats, mix well, then stir in yeast mixture. Gradually
add enough flour to make a stiff dough and knead for 5 to 10
minutes until smooth and elastic. Place in buttered bowl, turn to
grease top, cover, and let rise until doubled. Punch down, divide in
half, press into 2 greased 8½-inch loaf pans, and let rise again until
doubled. Bake in preheated 350° oven for about 50 minutes. (If
desired, mix a tablespoon of water with an egg white and brush over
tops of loaves before baking.) *Makes 2 loaves.*

COUNTRY BREAD

A good-tasting, easy-to-make bread well suited for beginning bakers.

1½ cups warm water
¼ cup sugar
1 cup oats or cornmeal or
   wheat germ
1 package dry yeast

2 teaspoons salt
2 egg yolks
⅓ cup corn oil
1 cup dry milk
4 cups flour

Mix warm water, sugar, and oats in large bowl. Sprinkle in yeast and set aside for 10 minutes. Stir in salt, egg yolks, corn oil, dry milk, and flour. Cover and let rise in warm place for 30 minutes. Stir or work dough with your hands (it will be sticky) for a few minutes, then let rise again, covered. Divide dough between 2 greased 8½-inch loaf pans, pressing into pans with wooden spoon or your hands. Cover and let rise until dough reaches top of the pan. Place in a *cold* oven, turn oven to 350°, and put a shallow pan of water on bottom shelf of oven. Bake 40 to 45 minutes.   *Makes 2 loaves.*

LUELLA'S BROWN BREAD

Makes franks and beans something special.

2 packages dry yeast
1 teaspoon white sugar
½ cup warm water
⅓ cup rolled oats
⅔ cup cold water
¼ teaspoon salt
⅓ cup butter
2 cups water

1 tablespoon molasses
¾ cup white sugar
½ cup brown sugar
1½ teaspoons salt
1 cup graham or whole wheat
   flour
7 to 8 cups white flour

Dissolve yeast and 1 teaspoon white sugar in warm water and set aside. In saucepan combine oats, cold water, and ¼ teaspoon salt; bring to a boil, reduce heat, and simmer until thick. Add butter and stir until melted. Pour mixture into bread bowl. Add 2 cups water, molasses, sugars, 1½ teaspoons salt, and yeast mixture, and stir until smooth. Beat in flours, 1 cup at a time, to form a stiff dough. Turn out onto floured board and knead until smooth. Shape into a ball and place in large buttered bowl, turn to grease top, and let rise until doubled. Punch down, knead, and divide among 3 greased 9-inch loaf pans. Cover and let rise until doubled. Bake in preheated 325° oven 1 hour.   *Makes 3 loaves.*

JULIANA BREAD

Keep extra loaves on hand in the freezer.

2 packages dry yeast
½ cup warm water
1 cup rolled oats (quick or
  *regular)
1 cup raisins
1 tablespoon butter
2 cups boiling water

2 teaspoons salt
⅔ cup maple syrup
1 cup wheat germ
¼ cup dry cereal (any kind)
½ cup seeded dates, cut into
  thirds
4 cups flour

Dissolve yeast in warm water and set aside. In large bowl combine oats, raisins, and butter. Pour boiling water over mixture. Let cool slightly. Add salt, syrup, wheat germ, cereal, dates, and yeast. Beat in flour, 1 cup at a time, to form a stiff dough. Cover and let rise to top of bowl. Fill 2 greased 9-inch loaf pans ⅔ full. Do not cover. Let rise to tops of pans. Bake in preheated 400° oven 15 to 20 minutes. Lower heat to 300° and bake 30 to 40 minutes.   *Makes 2 loaves.*

RAISIN BREAD

Soaking the raisins helps to keep them moist, even after the dough bakes.

1 package dry yeast
¼ cup warm water
1¾ cups milk
½ cup sugar
4 tablespoons butter (½ stick)
2 teaspoons salt
5½ to 6½ cups flour

Melted butter
2 cups raisins, soaked 1 hour
  in boiling water or
  overnight in sherry,
  drained
1 egg yolk
1 tablespoon milk

Dissolve yeast in warm water and set aside. Scald 1¾ cups milk, add sugar, butter, and salt, and stir until butter melts. Cool. Add yeast mixture and beat in flour, 1 cup at a time, to form a stiff dough. Turn out onto floured board and knead until smooth. Place in buttered bowl, turn to grease top, cover, and let rise until doubled. Punch down, turn out onto floured board, and knead several minutes. Return to bowl, cover, and let rise 45 minutes. Divide dough into 2 equal pieces and roll each out into a rectangle about 8 inches wide, ¼ inch thick. Brush with melted butter and sprinkle with raisins. Starting at a short end, roll up tightly and place seam-side down in 2 greased 8-inch loaf pans. Cover and let rise until doubled. Combine egg yolk and 1 tablespoon milk, and brush on tops of loaves. Bake in preheated 375° oven 30 to 40 minutes.   *Makes 2 loaves.*

RAISIN APPLE BREAD

Serve toasted or plain, with peanut butter, jam, or cream cheese.

2 packages dry yeast
¼ cup warm water
1½ cups milk
¼ cup sugar
½ teaspoon salt

1 egg, beaten
½ cup wheat germ
1 cup raisins
1 cup peeled, chopped apple
4 to 5 cups flour

Dissolve yeast in warm water and set aside. Scald milk, remove from heat, and stir in sugar and salt. Pour into bread bowl and, when cool, add yeast and egg. Beat in wheat germ, raisins, and apple. Add flour, 1 cup at a time, to form a stiff dough. Turn out onto floured board and knead until smooth. Place in buttered bowl, turn to grease top, cover, and let rise until doubled. Punch down and place in 2 greased 9-inch loaf pans. Cover and let rise until doubled. Bake in preheated 375° oven 30 to 35 minutes.   *Makes 2 loaves.*

RAISED PRUNE BREAD

Perfect for breakfast or brunch.

1 package dry yeast
¼ cup warm water
½ cup milk
2 tablespoons butter
2 tablespoons white sugar
½ teaspoon salt
1 egg
3 cups flour

2 tablespoons melted butter
2 cups cooked, pitted,
    chopped prunes (1 pound)
¼ cup brown sugar
1 teaspoon cinnamon
2 tablespoons lemon juice

Dissolve yeast in warm water and set aside. Scald milk, add butter, and stir until melted. When cool, beat in white sugar, salt, and egg. In bread bowl combine yeast and milk mixtures. Beat in flour, 1 cup at a time, to form a soft dough. Turn out onto floured board and knead until smooth. Shape into a ball, place in buttered bowl, turn to grease top, cover, and let rise until doubled. Roll out into rectangle approximately 9x16 inches. Brush with the melted butter. In a small bowl combine prunes, brown sugar, cinnamon, and lemon juice. Spread on top of dough. Roll up into tight jelly roll, shape into ring, and place in greased tube pan. Cover and let rise 30 minutes. Bake in preheated 350° oven 40 to 50 minutes.   *Makes 1 ring.*

BRIOCHE

Makes one loaf of rich bread, or two dozen rolls.

½ cup milk	1 teaspoon salt
1 cup butter (2 sticks)	4 cups flour
1 package dry yeast	4 eggs
1 tablespoon sugar	Melted butter

Scald milk, add butter, and stir until melted. Pour mixture into bread bowl. When cool, add yeast, sugar, and salt. Beat in 1 cup flour, 1 egg, and repeat until all are added to form a sticky dough. Turn out onto floured board and knead until smooth. (Work in additional flour as necessary.) Shape dough into a ball, place in buttered bowl, turn to grease top, cover, and let rise until doubled. Punch down. Pull off about 1 cup dough and shape into round ball. Shape remaining dough into larger ball. Place large ball in buttered 1½-quart soufflé dish. Cut a 2-inch slit in the center of the top and insert small ball in opening so two are joined. Brush top of entire shape with melted butter. Cover and let rise until doubled. Bake in preheated 375° oven 40 minutes. *Makes 1 loaf.*

To make rolls: Divide dough into 12 larger and 12 smaller pieces, shape into balls, and join as directed above. Brush with butter and bake in greased muffin pans 20 minutes.

SALLY LUNN

A traditional way to make this New England favorite.

1 package dry yeast	3 eggs
½ cup warm milk	4 cups flour
½ cup butter (1 stick)	Sugar
⅓ cup sugar	

Dissolve yeast in warm milk. Cream butter and sugar. Beat in eggs. Sift in flour, 1 cup at a time, adding alternately with yeast mixture to form a smooth dough. Cover and let rise until doubled. Punch down, beat well, and place in 2 greased 7-inch loaf pans. Cover and let rise until doubled. Sprinkle with sugar and bake in preheated 350° oven 20 minutes. *Makes 2 loaves.*

CROWN BREAD

Named for its beautiful shape.

2 packages dry yeast
½ cup warm water
1½ cups milk
4 tablespoons butter (½ stick)

3 tablespoons sugar
1½ teaspoons salt
6 to 8 cups flour
Melted butter

Dissolve yeast in warm water and set aside. Scald milk, add butter, sugar, and salt, and stir until butter melts. Cool. Add yeast and beat in flour, 1 cup at a time, to form a stiff dough. Turn out onto floured board and knead until smooth. Shape into ball, place in buttered bowl, turn to grease top, cover, and let rise until doubled. Punch down and shape into 30 to 34 small balls (about the size of Ping-Pong balls). Arrange half the balls in a well-greased, 10-inch tube pan. Brush with melted butter, arrange remaining balls on top of these, and brush with butter. Cover and let rise until doubled. Bake in preheated 375° oven 35 to 45 minutes. *Makes 1 loaf.*

MONKEY BREAD

Children love this bread, perhaps because of its name.

2 packages dry yeast
1 teaspoon sugar
¼ cup warm water
¾ cup milk
½ cup butter (1 stick)

⅓ cup sugar
1 teaspoon salt
5 cups flour
3 eggs
Melted butter

Dissolve yeast and 1 teaspoon sugar in warm water and set aside. Scald milk, add butter, ⅓ cup sugar, and salt, and stir until butter melts. Cool. Add yeast mixture and 2½ cups flour. Beat in eggs and add remaining 2½ cups flour to form a soft, but not sticky, dough. Turn out onto floured board and knead until smooth. Place in buttered bowl, turn to grease top, cover, and let rise until doubled. Punch down and turn out onto floured board. Roll out to ¼-inch thickness. Cut dough into diamonds or any shape desired. Or, don't roll out but shape dough into 1½-inch-diameter balls. Dip each piece into melted butter and arrange in a 10-inch tube pan. Cover and let rise until doubled. Bake in preheated 375° oven 45 minutes or until brown. *Makes 1 loaf.*

NUT ROLL

Rich, moist, and sweet.

2 packages dry yeast
½ cup warm milk
1 tablespoon sugar
6½ to 7 cups flour
¾ cup sugar
1 teaspoon salt

1 cup milk, scalded and
    slightly cooled
2 eggs, beaten
4 egg yolks, beaten
½ cup softened butter (1 stick)
Melted butter

Dissolve yeast in ½ cup warm milk. Add 1 tablespoon sugar and set aside. Sift together 6½ cups flour, ¾ cup sugar, and salt into a large bowl. Make a well in the center and add cooled scalded milk, eggs, yolks, butter, and yeast mixture. Mix thoroughly with wooden spoon and knead in bowl until no longer sticky. Add ½ cup more flour if necessary. Form into a soft ball and place in greased bowl. Cover with wax paper and damp cloth, and let rise until doubled. Make filling (see below) as dough rises. Punch down and place on floured cloth. Roll out to ¼-inch thickness (about 22x36 inches). Spread filling evenly on top of dough, leaving several inches of plain dough around the edges. Sprinkle top of filling with raisins, if desired, and generously sprinkle with sugar.

Lift long side of dough with cloth and coax to roll as a jelly roll. After dough is completely rolled, cut with floured spatula (to seal ends) into four 9-inch pieces; pinch seam of dough closed. Place seam-side down in 4 greased 9-inch bread pans. Prick dough on top with toothpicks to prevent bubbles. Cover with cloth and let rise 45 minutes. Brush tops with melted butter and bake in preheated 325° oven 45 to 60 minutes, or until a toothpick inserted in the center comes out clean. *Makes 4 loaves.*

NUT FILLING

1 cup cream
½ cup butter (1 stick)
½ cup honey
4 cups ground walnuts
1 teaspoon grated lemon peel
1 teaspoon vanilla
1 teaspoon salt

2 egg yolks
1 cup sour cream
2 egg whites, beaten until stiff
1¾ cups sugar
1 cup golden raisins
    (optional)

Scald together cream, butter, and honey, and pour over nuts. Stir in lemon peel, vanilla, and salt. Fold in egg yolks, sour cream, and egg whites. Blend in sugar and use filling as directed above.

CINNAMON SWIRL BREAD

The taste matches the aroma of this bread as it bakes.

2 packages dry yeast	3 eggs
1 cup warm water	6 to 7 cups flour
¾ cup milk	Melted butter
⅓ cup butter	½ cup sugar
5 tablespoons sugar	3 teaspoons cinnamon
1 teaspoon salt	1 egg white, lightly beaten

Dissolve yeast in warm water and set aside. Scald milk, add butter, 5 tablespoons sugar, and salt, and stir until butter melts. Cool. Beat in eggs. Add flour, 1 cup at a time, to form a stiff dough. Turn out onto floured board and knead until smooth. Shape into a ball, place in buttered bowl, turn to grease top, cover, and let rise until doubled. Punch down and divide in half. Roll out each piece into a rectangle approximately 8x16 inches. Brush each with melted butter. Combine ½ cup sugar with cinnamon, and sprinkle each piece with half of the mixture. Roll up tightly and place in 2 greased 9-inch loaf pans. Cover and let rise until doubled. Bake in preheated 375° oven 35 to 45 minutes. *Makes 2 loaves.*

PORTUGUESE SWEET BREAD

Rich but not too sweet, this bread comes from Provincetown's Portuguese community.

2 packages dry yeast	1 teaspoon salt
¼ cup warm water	7 to 8 eggs
½ cup milk	1 cup softened butter (2 sticks)
½ cup sugar	Milk
6 cups flour	

Dissolve yeast in warm water and set aside. Scald milk and stir in sugar. Let cool. In bread bowl mix 4 cups flour, salt, and yeast and milk mixtures. Beat in eggs, 1 at a time, until blended. Add 1 more cup flour. Beat in butter, 3 tablespoons at a time. Place dough on floured surface and knead in remaining 1 cup flour to form a smooth dough. Knead 10 to 15 minutes. Shape into a ball. Place in buttered bowl, turn to grease top, cover, and let rise until doubled. Punch down, divide in half, and pat into 2 round loaves. Place on greased baking sheet, cover, and let rise until doubled. Brush tops with cold milk and bake in preheated 350° oven 40 to 50 minutes.

Makes 2 loaves.

CHRISTMAS BREAD

A nice gift for your neighbors.

1 cup candied fruits
1 cup raisins or currants
½ cup candied red or green
    cherries (or mixture of
    both)
⅔ cup rum
2 packages dry yeast
½ cup warm water
1 cup milk
¾ cup butter

½ cup sugar
½ teaspoon salt
½ teaspoon almond extract
3 eggs
6 to 7 cups flour
Melted butter

Combine candied fruits, raisins, cherries, and rum, and let sit 1 to 2 hours. Drain, reserving rum. Dissolve yeast in warm water and set aside. Scald milk, add butter, sugar, and salt, and stir until butter melts. Cool. In bread bowl combine milk and yeast mixtures, reserved rum, almond extract, and eggs. Beat in 2 cups flour, then 1 cup fruit, and continue until all are added. Turn out onto floured board and knead until smooth. Shape into a ball, place in buttered bowl, turn to grease top, cover, and let rise until doubled. Punch down and divide in half. On floured board roll each out into rectangle about 8x14 inches. Brush each with melted butter, and fold into thirds the long way, bringing edges to overlap in middle by 2 inches. Press each edge down to secure it. Place loaves on greased baking sheet, cover, and let rise until doubled. Bake in preheated 375° oven 30 to 40 minutes. Remove to racks to cool. Sprinkle with powdered sugar, or frost with Almond or White Icing (see page 134) and sprinkle with chopped pecans. *Makes 2 loaves.*

ITALIAN EASTER BREAD

A springtime treat in Italian communities from Maine to Rhode Island.

1 cup warm water	½ cup melted butter (1 stick)
¾ cup sugar	4½ to 5 cups sifted flour
1 teaspoon salt	4 uncooked eggs, colored
1 package dry yeast	Melted butter
2 eggs, beaten	

Combine water, sugar, and salt in bowl. Sprinkle yeast into mixture and stir until dissolved. Add 2 eggs, ½ cup melted butter, and 2½ cups flour. Beat with wooden spoon. Add enough additional flour to form a stiff dough. Turn out onto floured board and knead until smooth. Shape into a ball, place in buttered bowl, turn to grease top, cover, and let rise until doubled. Divide dough into 3 equal parts. Cover and let rise 10 minutes. Knead each gently 1 minute. Roll out into 3 ropes, each about 20 inches long. Braid together and place on greased baking sheet. Shape into a ring by pinching ends firmly together. Tuck colored, uncooked eggs into braid. Brush braid lightly with melted butter and place greased custard cup in center of ring. Cover and let rise 30 minutes. Remove custard cup. Bake in preheated 425° oven 25 minutes. Remove to rack. When cool, dust lightly with powdered sugar. *Makes 1 ring.*

EASTER BABA

This fine-textured bread, a holiday specialty for New Englanders of Polish heritage, is baked in a fluted pan to resemble a woman's skirt.

3 packages dry yeast	1 cup softened butter (2 sticks)
1 cup warm milk	1 teaspoon vanilla
1 teaspoon salt	¼ teaspoon almond extract
15 egg yolks	3 tablespoons dry bread
4 cups flour	crumbs
1 cup sugar	

Dissolve yeast in warm milk and set aside. Add salt to egg yolks and beat until thick and lemon colored. Add yeast mixture and 2 cups flour, and mix well. Cover and let rise until doubled. Punch down and add remaining flour, sugar, butter, and flavorings. Beat until dough falls away from spoon. Cover and let rise until doubled. Punch down, cover, and let rise again. Punch down, divide in half, and place each piece in a greased 9-inch tube pan that has been sprinkled with half the bread crumbs. Cover and let rise until doubled. Bake in preheated 350° oven 40 minutes. *Makes 2 loaves.*

III.
Quick Breads

WHOLE WHEAT-APPLE BREAD

A mixer with a dough hook helps in stirring the stiff dough for this moist bread.

½ cup melted butter (1 stick)
1 cup brown sugar
2 eggs
1½ cups milk
½ cup white flour
1 tablespoon baking powder

2 cups whole wheat flour
1 cup wheat germ
1 cup chopped raisins
1 cup chopped apple
   (unpeeled)

Preheat oven to 350°. Beat together butter, brown sugar, eggs, and milk. Sift together white flour and baking powder. Add whole wheat flour, wheat germ, raisins, and apple. Beat flour mixture into egg mixture to form a stiff dough. Spoon into greased 8½-inch loaf pan and bake 50 to 60 minutes. *Makes 1 loaf.*

APPLESAUCE BREAD

Adjust sugar according to the sweetness of the applesauce.

2 cups flour
¼ cup sugar
1 tablespoon baking powder
¼ teaspoon salt
½ teaspoon baking soda
1 teaspoon cinnamon

1 egg
1 cup applesauce
4 tablespoons melted butter
   (½ stick)
¼ cup chopped nuts
1 cup currants or raisins

Preheat oven to 350°. Sift together dry ingredients. Beat together egg, applesauce, and butter. Add sifted ingredients and stir to mix. Fold in nuts and currants. Bake in greased 9-inch loaf pan 50 to 60 minutes. *Makes 1 loaf.*

APRICOT-APPLESAUCE BREAD

Serve this when company comes.

3½ cups flour
½ cup sugar
1 tablespoon baking powder
½ teaspoon salt
½ teaspoon baking soda
½ teaspoon cinnamon

2 eggs, beaten
1½ cups applesauce
4 tablespoons melted butter
   (½ stick)
1 cup chopped, dried apricots

Preheat oven to 350°. Sift together flour, sugar, baking powder, salt, soda, and cinnamon. Stir together eggs, applesauce, and butter, and add to dry ingredients. Stir until blended. Fold in apricots. Pour into greased 8-inch loaf pan and bake 50 to 60 minutes. Cool in pan.

Makes 1 loaf.

APRICOT BREAD

Peach jam or orange marmalade can also be used.

1 egg
4 tablespoons melted butter
   (½ stick)
¾ cup apricot juice
2 cups apricot preserves

3 cups flour
1 tablespoon baking powder
1 teaspoon baking soda
¼ teaspoon salt
1 cup chopped nuts

Preheat oven to 350°. Beat together egg and butter. Mix in apricot juice and 1¾ cups of the preserves. Sift together flour, baking powder, soda, and salt. Blend dry ingredients into wet and stir until smooth. Fold in nuts. Bake in greased 9-inch loaf pan 50 to 60 minutes. Remove from oven, let sit 5 minutes, and turn out onto baking sheet. Spread top with remaining ¼ cup preserves and return to oven 5 minutes to glaze.

Makes 1 loaf.

BANANA BREAD

Use very ripe bananas and bake as a cake.

1¼ cups flour
¾ cup sugar
¼ teaspoon salt
1 teaspoon baking soda

½ cup shortening or lard
1 cup mashed bananas
2 eggs

Preheat oven to 350°. Sift together flour, sugar, salt, and soda. Cut in shortening until mixture is crumbly. Beat together bananas and eggs. Fold dry ingredients into banana mixture and stir just until flour is moistened. Bake in greased and floured 9-inch square cake pan 40 to 45 minutes. Let stand in pan 10 minutes, then turn out on rack to cool. *Makes 16 squares.*

BUTTERMILK BANANA BREAD

This loaf will store well in the freezer.

½ cup softened butter (1 stick)
½ cup brown sugar
3 ripe bananas, mashed

¼ cup buttermilk
1 teaspoon baking soda
½ teaspoon salt
2¼ cups flour

Preheat oven to 350°. Cream butter, brown sugar, and bananas. Add buttermilk and stir until blended. Sift together dry ingredients and stir into banana mixture. Bake in greased 8-inch loaf pan 50 to 60 minutes. *Makes 1 loaf.*

CRANBERRY-BANANA BREAD

Easy to slice and good served plain.

3 tablespoons butter
¾ cup sugar
1 egg
2 cups flour
2 tablespoons baking powder

½ teaspoon salt
1 cup mashed banana
¼ cup milk
1½ cups chopped cranberries
1 cup chopped walnuts

Preheat oven to 350°. Cream butter and sugar. Beat in egg. Sift together flour, baking powder, and salt. Combine banana and milk. Add dry mixture and banana mixture to creamed mixture and stir until smooth. Add cranberries and nuts, and mix well. Pour into greased 9-inch loaf pan. Bake 50 to 60 minutes. *Makes 1 loaf.*

MOLASSES BANANA BREAD

Puree bananas in the blender, or mash well.

3 ripe bananas, mashed
1 egg
½ cup sugar
3 tablespoons molasses
2 tablespoons melted butter

2 cups flour
1 teaspoon baking soda
1 teaspoon baking powder
½ teaspoon salt

Preheat oven to 350°. Beat together bananas, egg, sugar, molasses, and butter. Sift together dry ingredients and stir into banana mixture. Bake in greased 8-inch loaf pan 50 to 60 minutes.

Makes 1 loaf.

RAISIN BANANA BREAD

Add half a cup of nuts for a more dense, fruitcake-type bread.

½ cup butter (1 stick)
½ cup sugar
2 eggs
2 ripe bananas, mashed
¼ cup buttermilk

2 cups flour
1 teaspoon baking soda
½ teaspoon salt
½ cup raisins

Preheat oven to 325°. Cream butter and sugar. Beat in eggs and bananas. Add buttermilk and beat until smooth. Sift together flour, soda, and salt, and add, along with raisins, to banana mixture. Stir quickly, just enough to moisten dry ingredients. Bake in greased 9-inch loaf pan 1 hour. Let sit 5 minutes, remove from pan, and cool on rack.

Makes 1 loaf.

BLUEBERRY BREAD

Use fresh or dry-frozen berries.

2½ cups flour
1 teaspoon baking soda
2 teaspoons baking powder
½ teaspoon cinnamon
½ teaspoon salt
½ cup sugar

2 tablespoons melted butter
1 cup buttermilk
1 egg
1 cup blueberries
½ cup chopped nuts

Preheat oven to 350°. Sift together flour, soda, baking powder, cinnamon, and salt. In bread bowl combine sugar, butter, buttermilk, and egg, and beat until smooth. Stir in dry ingredients, and add blueberries and nuts. Bake in greased 8-inch loaf pan 50 to 60 minutes.

Makes 1 loaf.

COCONUT BREAD

This is best made with fresh coconut, but packaged coconut can be used as a last resort as long as you rinse it with warm water to remove the sugar.

4 cups flour	1 cup milk
1¼ cups sugar	1 egg, beaten
1 teaspoon salt	2 teaspoons vanilla
4 teaspoons baking powder	3 cups grated fresh coconut*
2 tablespoons butter	

Combine flour, sugar, salt, and baking powder in large bowl. Mix well. Melt butter, cool, and add to milk. Stir in egg and vanilla. Add to flour mixture along with coconut and use hands to blend as batter will be very stiff. Press into greased 9-inch loaf pan, cover, let rise for 45 minutes, then bake in preheated 350° oven for 1¾ hours.

Makes 1 loaf.

*Crack open coconut, remove meat, leaving on brown inner skin, and grate on metal grater. One coconut yields about 4 cups grated.

TART CRANBERRY BREAD

Serve this colorful bread with turkey or chicken salad.

2½ cups flour	1 cup orange juice
½ cup sugar	2 tablespoons grated orange
1 teaspoon baking powder	rind
½ teaspoon baking soda	1 egg, beaten
½ teaspoon salt	2½ cups chopped cranberries
¼ cup shortening	

Preheat oven to 350°. Sift together flour, sugar, baking powder, soda, and salt. Cut in shortening until mixture is crumbly. In separate bowl blend orange juice, orange rind, and egg. Mix in dry ingredients. Fold in cranberries. Spoon into greased 8-inch loaf pan. Bake 50 to 60 minutes. Remove from pan and cool. *Makes 1 loaf.*

CRANBERRY-CURRANT BREAD

Makes delicious toast.

Juice of 1 lemon
1 cup water
½ cup currants
½ cup brown sugar
2 cups flour
2 teaspoons baking powder

¼ teaspoon baking soda
½ teaspoon salt
2 tablespoons melted butter
1 egg
½ cup chopped cranberries

Preheat oven to 350°. Combine lemon juice, water, currants, and brown sugar in saucepan and simmer 5 minutes. Set aside to cool. Sift together flour, baking powder, soda, and salt. Beat together butter and egg. Add to dry ingredients along with currant mixture. Stir until well blended. Fold in cranberries. Pour into greased 8-inch loaf pan and bake 40 to 50 minutes. *Makes 1 loaf.*

CRANBERRY-CHEESE BREAD

Use a sharp cheddar in this fragrant loaf.

3 cups flour
½ cup sugar
2 teaspoons baking powder
2 teaspoons baking soda
Rind of 1 large orange, grated
4 tablespoons butter (½ stick)

Juice of orange, plus water to
    equal 1 cup
2 eggs
1 cup grated cheddar cheese
2 cups chopped cranberries

Preheat oven to 350°. Sift together flour, sugar, baking powder, and soda. Add orange rind and cut in butter. Beat together liquid and eggs, and add to dry ingredients along with cheese and cranberries. If batter seems dry, add more juice or water. Pour into greased 9-inch loaf pan and bake 50 to 60 minutes. Cool overnight on rack before slicing. *Makes 1 loaf.*

DATE BREAD

A moist, heavy bread that may need to bake more than an hour.

2 cups whole wheat flour
1 cup rye flour
2 cups white flour
2 teaspoons baking powder
1 teaspoon salt

½ cup sugar
1 cup chopped dates
3 cups buttermilk
2 tablespoons melted butter

In large bowl sift together dry ingredients. Beat in dates, buttermilk, and butter. Pour into 2 greased 8-inch loaf pans and let sit, covered, in warm place for 20 minutes. Bake in preheated 350° oven 50 to 60 minutes.   *Makes 2 loaves.*

DATE BEAN BREAD

An unusual bread that contains cooked beans for added nutrition and substance.

1 egg
⅓ cup melted butter
⅓ cup white sugar
⅓ cup brown sugar
1 cup chopped dates
½ cup milk
1 cup cooked pinto beans,
    drained and mashed

1 teaspoon cinnamon
1 teaspoon salt
1½ cups flour
1 teaspoon baking powder
½ teaspoon baking soda
½ cup chopped nuts

Preheat oven to 350°. Combine first 7 ingredients in bread bowl. Sift together dry ingredients and add to egg mixture, blending well. Fold in nuts and turn into greased 9-inch loaf pan. Bake 40 minutes. Remove from oven and let sit 10 minutes. Cool on rack.

Makes 1 loaf.

HOLIDAY FRUIT BREAD

Simpler than a fruitcake, but just as festive.

2 cups white flour
4 teaspoons baking powder
1 teaspoon salt
½ cup sugar
2 cups graham flour
½ cup chopped candied
   orange peel

¼ cup chopped cranberries
1 cup chopped walnuts
1½ cups milk
2 eggs
4 tablespoons melted butter
   (½ stick)

Preheat oven to 350°. Sift together white flour, baking powder, salt, and sugar. Stir in graham flour, orange peel, cranberries, and walnuts. Beat together milk, eggs, and butter, and stir into dry ingredients. (Add a bit more milk if batter seems dry.) Pour into 2 greased 7-inch loaf pans. Bake 50 to 60 minutes. Cool on racks.

Makes 2 loaves.

LEMON BREAD

Serve as a tea bread with cream cheese.

½ cup softened butter (1 stick)
¾ cup sugar
Rind of 1 lemon, grated
2 eggs
1½ cups flour

1½ teaspoons baking powder
½ teaspoon salt
½ cup milk
Juice of 1 lemon
¼ to ½ cup sugar

Preheat oven to 350°. Cream butter and ¾ cup sugar. Add lemon rind and eggs, and beat well. Sift together flour, baking powder, and salt. Add to butter mixture along with milk and stir until dry ingredients are just moistened. Bake in greased 9-inch loaf pan 50 to 60 minutes. When done, remove from oven. Mix together lemon juice and sugar to taste and pour over hot bread. Let bread sit in pan to cool.

Makes 1 loaf.

ORANGE BREAD I

It's easy to undercook this bread, so be sure to test it carefully before removing it from the oven.

2 tablespoons softened butter
1 cup sugar
1 egg, slightly beaten
¾ cup orange juice
2 tablespoons grated orange rind
2 cups sifted flour

½ teaspoon baking soda
1 teaspoon baking powder
½ teaspoon salt
½ cup coarsely chopped pecans
½ cup finely sliced dates

Preheat oven to 350°. Cream butter and sugar, then add egg, juice, and rind, and mix until well blended. Sift together flour, soda, baking powder, and salt, and stir into creamed mixture. Mix in nuts and dates. Pour into 2 greased 7-inch loaf pans and bake for 50 minutes, or until a toothpick inserted in the center of the loaf comes out clean. *Makes 2 loaves.*

ORANGE BREAD II

A dense loaf flavored with orange juice and peel.

3 cups whole wheat flour
1 cup sugar
4 teaspoons baking powder
¾ teaspoon salt

1 egg
1 cup orange juice
¼ cup grated orange peel
⅓ cup melted butter

Preheat oven to 350°. Sift together flour, sugar, baking powder, and salt. Beat egg slightly and beat in juice, peel, and cooled butter. Combine mixtures and beat until well blended. Bake in greased 9-inch loaf pan for 30 to 40 minutes. Turn out and cool on rack. *Makes 1 loaf.*

ORANGE MARMALADE BREAD

This has a wonderful orange flavor and is always moist.

1 egg, beaten
4 tablespoons melted butter
  (½ stick)
1 jar (16 ounces) orange
  marmalade
¾ cup orange juice

3 cups flour
3 teaspoons baking powder
1 teaspoon baking soda
¼ teaspoon salt
1 cup chopped nuts

Preheat oven to 350°. Mix egg and cooled butter and beat well. Add marmalade, minus ¼ cup, and orange juice. Sift together dry ingredients and add to egg mixture along with nuts. Pour into greased 9½-inch loaf pan and bake for 1 hour or until toothpick inserted comes out clean. Remove from oven and turn out onto baking sheet. Spread with ¼ cup reserved marmalade, covering top. Return to oven about 2 minutes or until nicely glazed. Cool before cutting.   *Makes 1 loaf.*

PINEAPPLE BREAD

Use canned pineapple rather than fresh.

3 cups flour
½ teaspoon cinnamon
1 tablespoon baking powder
1 teaspoon baking soda
½ teaspoon salt
2 eggs

¼ cup water
½ cup melted butter (1 stick)
½ cup honey
1 cup (8-ounce can) crushed
  pineapple, undrained

Preheat oven to 350°. Sift together dry ingredients. Beat together eggs, water, butter, and honey. Stir in pineapple and blend in dry ingredients. Bake in greased 9-inch loaf pan 50 to 60 minutes.
                                                    Makes 1 loaf.

PINEAPPLE AND CHEESE BREAD

An unusual bread that will be the attraction at any party. Serve plain with tea or coffee.

2 cups flour
¾ cup sugar
3 teaspoons baking powder
½ teaspoon baking soda
1 teaspoon salt
1 egg

1 can (8 ounces) crushed
  pineapple, undrained
2 tablespoons melted butter
½ cup grated sharp cheddar
  cheese
½ cup coarsely chopped nuts

Preheat oven to 350°. Sift together flour, sugar, baking powder, soda, and salt. Beat egg lightly and stir in pineapple and cooled melted butter. Add dry ingredients and stir quickly until all are moistened; then lightly stir in cheese and nuts. Turn into greased 9-inch loaf pan and bake for 1 hour or until done. Cool completely before slicing. *Makes 1 loaf.*

PINEAPPLE NUT BREAD

Excellent taste, texture, and appearance.

4 teaspoons baking soda
1 can (20 ounces) crushed
  pineapple, undrained
2 eggs
2 teaspoons vanilla
¾ cup melted butter (1½
  sticks)

4 cups flour
1 cup sugar
1 teaspoon salt
2 cups raisins
1 cup chopped nuts

Preheat oven to 350°. Mix 2 teaspoons soda with pineapple and set aside. Beat eggs and add vanilla, cooled butter, pineapple mixture, flour, sugar, remaining 2 teaspoons soda, salt, raisins, and nuts. Pour into 2 greased 9-inch loaf pans and bake for 1 hour and 15 minutes. *Makes 2 loaves.*

PRUNE BREAD

The Madeira makes this extra-special.

1 teaspoon grated lemon peel
1½ cups pitted, diced prunes
½ cup Madeira
2 eggs
½ cup milk

2½ cups flour
¼ cup sugar
1 teaspoon cinnamon
3 teaspoons baking powder

Soak lemon peel and prunes in Madeira overnight. Drain, reserving liquid. Combine eggs, milk, and prune liquid in bread bowl. Sift together flour, sugar, cinnamon, and baking powder, and add to liquid. Blend in lemon peel and prunes. Pour mixture into greased soufflé dish. Bake at 350° for 50 minutes or until browned. Remove from oven, let cool, and turn onto rack.   *Makes 1 loaf.*

STRAWBERRY BREAD

Store in the refrigerator after cooling, and serve with homemade strawberry jam.

2 cups flour
½ cup light brown sugar
1 tablespoon baking powder
1 teaspoon baking soda
3 tablespoons butter

1 egg
2 cups fresh or frozen
  strawberries, mashed
2 teaspoons grated lemon rind

Preheat oven to 350°. Sift together flour, brown sugar, baking powder, and soda. Beat together butter and egg. Stir dry ingredients into butter mixture until blended. Add berries and lemon rind and stir well. Bake in greased 8-inch loaf pan 50 to 60 minutes. Let cool 5 minutes, and remove to rack.   *Makes 1 loaf.*

JAM BREAD

An old-time recipe for putting jam into bread. You can use jelly or marmalade as well.

3 cups flour
1 tablespoon baking powder
½ teaspoon salt
½ teaspoon baking soda
1 egg
½ cup fruit juice (cranberry, orange, etc.)

1¼ cups jam
4 tablespoons melted butter (½ stick)
1 cup chopped walnuts

Preheat oven to 350°. Sift together dry ingredients. Beat in egg, juice, 1 cup jam, and butter. Stir in nuts. Pour into greased 9-inch loaf pan and bake 50 to 60 minutes. Spread top with remaining jam and return to oven for 5 minutes to glaze. Or, add all the jam to batter and frost with White Icing (see page 134). *Makes 1 loaf.*

CARROT CURRANT BREAD

Slices best the day after it is baked.

6 tablespoons butter
⅔ cup sugar
2 eggs
1½ cups flour
1½ teaspoons baking powder
½ teaspoon cinnamon

½ teaspoon nutmeg
½ teaspoon salt
1 cup peeled, grated carrots
1 cup currants
½ cup chopped pecans

Preheat oven to 350°. Cream butter and sugar. Beat in eggs. Sift together flour, baking powder, cinnamon, nutmeg, and salt. Stir dry ingredients into butter mixture. Blend in carrots, currants, and pecans. Bake in greased 8-inch loaf pan 50 to 60 minutes. Let sit in pan 15 minutes, then turn out onto rack to cool. *Makes 1 loaf.*

CARROT AND WHEAT GERM BREAD

A spicy, moist, coarse-textured bread.

1 cup whole wheat flour
1 cup wheat germ
½ teaspoon salt
¼ teaspoon freshly grated
    nutmeg
½ cup chopped walnuts
¼ cup brown sugar
2 teaspoons baking powder

2 eggs
6 tablespoons melted butter
½ cup freshly squeezed orange
    juice
½ cup peeled, grated potatoes
1½ cups peeled, grated carrots

Preheat oven to 425°. Combine flour, wheat germ, salt, nutmeg, walnuts, brown sugar, and baking powder. Beat together eggs, butter, and orange juice, and add to dry ingredients, stirring to form a soft batter. Mix in potatoes and carrots. Pour batter into greased 9-inch loaf pan and bake 10 minutes. Reduce heat to 325° and bake 40 to 50 minutes longer. *Makes 1 loaf.*

SPICY PUMPKIN BREAD

Present this sweet, dense bread at brunch, lunch, or dinner.

3 eggs
1 cup honey
2 cups pumpkin, canned, or
    cooked, mashed, and cooled
¼ cup oil
2 teaspoons baking soda
½ cup yogurt

¼ cup milk
4 cups flour
½ teaspoon salt
1 teaspoon nutmeg
1 teaspoon cinnamon

Preheat oven to 325°. Beat together eggs and honey. Add pumpkin and oil. Dissolve soda in yogurt and milk. Sift together flour, salt, nutmeg, and cinnamon, and add to pumpkin mixture along with yogurt. Beat well until blended. Pour into 2 greased 8-inch loaf pans and bake 1 to 1½ hours. *Makes 2 loaves.*

RHUBARB BREAD

One of the few quick or batter breads that can be served hot from the pan.

3 tablespoons butter
½ cup white sugar
1 cup chopped pecans
1 cup brown sugar
¾ cup melted butter
1 egg
1 cup buttermilk

1½ teaspoons baking soda
2¾ cups flour
½ teaspoon salt
2 cups chopped rhubarb,
    fresh, or frozen, thawed
    and drained
1 teaspoon vanilla

Preheat oven to 350°. Cut butter into white sugar until crumbly. Add ½ cup pecans and set aside. In separate bowl combine brown sugar, melted butter, egg, buttermilk, and soda. Sift in flour and salt, and stir until blended. Add rhubarb, vanilla, and remaining nuts. Pour into greased 9-inch loaf pan. Cover with reserved sugar and pecan mixture. Bake 45 minutes. *Makes 1 loaf.*

SQUASH BREAD

Serve this sweet bread with cream cheese.

½ cup white sugar
½ cup brown sugar
1 cup cooked, mashed winter
    squash (butternut, acorn, or
    Hubbard)
3 eggs
½ cup oil
½ teaspoon salt

2 teaspoons baking soda
2 cups flour
1 teaspoon cinnamon
½ teaspoon ginger
¼ cup milk
1 cup currants or raisins
½ cup chopped nuts

Preheat oven to 350°. Beat together sugars, squash, eggs, and oil. Sift together salt, soda, flour, cinnamon, and ginger. Add to squash mixture along with milk, currants, and nuts. Stir to form a smooth batter. Pour into greased 9-inch loaf pan and bake 50 to 60 minutes. Cool on rack. *Makes 1 loaf.*

TOMATO BREAD

An unorthodox use for an overabundance of fresh tomatoes.

1¼ cups milk
⅔ cup Grape-nuts cereal
½ teaspoon salt
1 tablespoon baking powder
2 cups flour
¼ to ½ cup sugar

4 tablespoons melted butter
(½ stick)
2 eggs, beaten
1 cup peeled, chopped
tomatoes

Preheat oven to 350°. Scald milk and pour over Grape-nuts. Set aside to cool. Sift together dry ingredients. Beat together butter and eggs, and blend in milk and Grape-nuts. Add dry ingredients and stir just until mixed. Fold in tomatoes. Place in greased 9-inch loaf pan and bake 50 to 60 minutes. Cool thoroughly and store overnight, wrapped in tinfoil, before slicing.   *Makes 1 loaf.*

ZUCCHINI BREAD

Many versions of this recipe produce a cake rather than a bread. Here's a recipe that makes something closer to bread.

1 cup sugar
½ cup oil
2 eggs
2 cups peeled, grated zucchini
2 teaspoons grated lemon rind
1 teaspoon vanilla
3 cups flour

2 teaspoons baking powder
1 teaspoon baking soda
½ teaspoon salt
½ teaspoon cinnamon
¾ cup chopped nuts
(optional)

Preheat oven to 350°. Beat together sugar, oil, and eggs. Add zucchini, lemon rind, and vanilla. Sift together flour, baking powder, soda, salt, and cinnamon. Beat into wet ingredients just enough to moisten. Stir in nuts, if used. Spoon into greased 9-inch loaf pan and bake 50 to 60 minutes. Cool on rack.   *Makes 1 loaf.*

CORN BREAD

This recipe can also be baked in a preheated, greased 8- or 9-inch cast-iron skillet.

1 cup cornmeal
1 cup flour
1 tablespoon baking powder
2 teaspoons sugar (or more to taste)

1 teaspoon salt
1 egg
1½ cups milk
4 tablespoons melted butter (½ stick)

Preheat oven to 425°. Sift together cornmeal, flour, baking powder, sugar, and salt. Beat together egg, milk, and butter, and add to dry ingredients, stirring until well blended. Pour into greased 8-inch square pan and bake 20 to 25 minutes. *Makes 16 squares.*

APPLE CORN BREAD

A little bit different from traditional corn bread.

1 cup cornmeal
1 cup flour
¾ cup sugar
1 tablespoon baking powder
1½ teaspoons salt
1 egg

1 cup milk
4 tablespoons melted butter (½ stick)
2 tart apples, cored and diced (unpeeled)

Preheat oven to 425°. Mix together dry ingredients. Beat together egg, milk, and butter, and add to dry ingredients along with apples, stirring just enough to moisten. Pour into greased 9-inch square pan and bake 20 to 25 minutes. *Makes 16 squares.*

HERB CORN BREAD

Slather with butter and honey.

1½ cups cornmeal
1 cup flour
2 teaspoons baking powder
¼ cup sugar
2 tablespoons chopped fresh
   herbs (dill, oregano,
   rosemary, chives, etc.)

½ teaspoon salt
2 eggs
4 tablespoons melted butter
   (½ stick)
1 cup milk (more or less)

Preheat oven to 400°. Combine cornmeal, flour, baking powder, sugar, herbs, and salt. Beat in eggs and butter. Add milk, enough so mixture is smooth but not thin. Pour into greased 9-inch square pan and bake 20 minutes.   *Makes 16 squares.*

PEANUT BUTTER CORN BREAD

Peanut butter lends a moist texture and a faintly nutty flavor to this corn bread variant.

1 cup flour
⅓ cup sugar
4 teaspoons baking powder
¾ teaspoon salt

1 cup cornmeal
1 cup milk
⅓ cup crunchy peanut butter
2 eggs

Preheat oven to 425°. Sift together flour, sugar, baking powder, and salt. Stir in cornmeal. Blend milk with peanut butter. Stir eggs into dry ingredients, then add milk mixture, stirring only enough to blend. Bake in greased 8-inch square pan for 20 to 25 minutes.
   Makes 12-16 squares.

PUMPKIN CORN BREAD

A dense, flavorful bread that tastes best the second day.

2 cups flour
1 tablespoon baking powder
½ teaspoon salt
½ cup sugar
1 cup cornmeal
4 tablespoons softened butter
  (½ stick)

2 eggs
2 cups (15-ounce can)
  pumpkin (or fresh
  pumpkin, steamed and
  strained)
1 small can (8 ounces) cream-
  style corn

Preheat oven to 350°. Sift together flour, baking powder, and salt. In separate bowl combine sugar, cornmeal, butter, and eggs, and stir in flour mixture until blended. Add pumpkin and corn. Pour into greased 9-inch loaf pan. Bake 1 hour or until center is firm. Cool 10 minutes and remove from pan. Let sit overnight before slicing.

Makes 1 loaf.

RICE CORN BREAD

A moist bread to serve warm, topped with lots of butter.

3 eggs, beaten
3 cups milk
2 cups cornmeal
1 cup cooked rice, cooled
1 tablespoon melted butter

1 teaspoon salt (less if rice
  cooked with salt)
1 tablespoon baking powder
½ teaspoon powdered sage

Preheat oven to 350°. Beat together eggs, milk, cornmeal, rice, butter, and salt. Add baking powder and sage, mix well, and pour into 2 well-greased 7-inch loaf pans. Bake 35 to 45 minutes. *Makes 2 loaves.*

SOUR MILK JOHNNYCAKE

This can be reheated the day after baking — if there's any left.

1½ cups flour
2 teaspoons baking powder
1 teaspoon salt
½ teaspoon baking soda
2 tablespoons sugar

1 cup cornmeal
2 eggs, beaten
1¼ cups buttermilk
3 tablespoons melted butter

Preheat oven to 425°. Sift together flour, baking powder, salt, soda, and sugar. Add cornmeal and stir. Combine eggs, buttermilk, and butter. Add to dry ingredients and mix well. Bake in greased 8-inch square pan 30 to 40 minutes. *Makes 16 squares.*

APPLESAUCE BROWN BREAD

Wonderful with baked beans.

1 cup applesauce
1 cup cornmeal
½ cup flour
½ cup whole wheat flour

1 teaspoon baking soda
1 teaspoon salt
¼ cup molasses
½ cup raisins

Combine all ingredients and stir until well blended. Grease the sides and bottom of a round, 1-pound coffee can. Pour in batter. Cover top tightly with tinfoil or wax paper tied on with string. Place can on rack inside a kettle and add warm water to come halfway up the side of can. Cover kettle, bring water to a boil, reduce heat, and simmer 2½ to 3 hours, or until bread is firm and a toothpick inserted in the center comes out clean. Add more water to kettle during baking as necessary. *Makes 1 loaf.*

BOSTON BROWN BREAD

If desired, add a cup of raisins to batter before baking.

1 cup cornmeal
1 cup graham flour
1 cup rye flour
1 cup molasses

1 cup buttermilk
2 teaspoons baking soda
½ teaspoon salt

Combine all ingredients and stir until well blended. Grease the sides and bottoms of 3 round, 1-pound coffee cans. Fill each with ⅓ of the batter. Cover tops tightly with tinfoil or wax paper tied on with string. Place cans on rack inside a kettle and add warm water to come halfway up the sides of cans. Cover kettle, bring water to a boil, reduce heat, and simmer 2½ to 3 hours, or until bread is firm and a toothpick inserted in the center comes out clean. Add more water to kettle during baking as necessary. *Makes 3 loaves.*

KAY'S BROWN BREAD

Another version of this Saturday night favorite.

1 cup flour	1 cup whole wheat flour
1 teaspoon baking powder	2 cups buttermilk
1 teaspoon baking soda	1 cup raisins
1 cup cornmeal	¾ cup dark molasses

Sift together flour, baking powder, and soda. Stir in cornmeal and whole wheat flour. Add buttermilk, raisins, and molasses. Beat well. Divide batter among 3 greased and floured 1-pound coffee cans. Cover tightly with tinfoil or wax paper tied on with string, and place on rack in deep kettle. Add boiling water to a depth of 1 inch. Cover and steam 3 hours, adding more boiling water as necessary. Remove cans from kettle, cool 10 minutes, and remove bread.

Makes 3 loaves.

MOLASSES BREAD

Somewhat akin to gingerbread, this loaf will slice best when cool.

4 tablespoons butter (½ stick)	1 tablespoon baking powder
¼ cup sugar	1 teaspoon salt
1 cup molasses	2 teaspoons baking soda
2 eggs	½ cup warm water
2 cups flour	

Preheat oven to 325°. Cream butter and sugar. Beat in molasses and eggs. Sift together flour, baking powder, and salt. Add to butter and molasses mixture. Combine soda and water and add. Pour mixture into greased 8-inch loaf pan and bake 50 to 60 minutes.

Makes 1 loaf.

QUICK SALLY LUNN

Serve warm with butter and jam.

6 tablespoons butter	2 cups flour
¼ cup sugar	4 teaspoons baking powder
2 eggs, beaten	½ teaspoon salt
1 cup milk	

Preheat oven to 425°. Cream butter and sugar. Beat in eggs and milk. Sift together flour, baking powder, and salt. Add butter and egg mixture to dry ingredients and beat until smooth. Turn into greased 8-inch square pan and bake 20 to 25 minutes. *Makes 16 squares.*

IRISH SODA BREAD

This can also be baked in a loaf pan.

4 cups flour
1 tablespoon baking soda
1 to 2 tablespoons sugar
2 teaspoons salt
2 tablespoons caraway seed
   (optional)

1 cup raisins or currants
   (optional)
2 cups buttermilk
Melted butter

Preheat oven to 375°. Sift together flour, soda, sugar, and salt. If used, blend in caraway seed and raisins, and mix until well floured. Stir in buttermilk to form a soft dough (like a biscuit dough). Turn out onto floured surface and knead gently 1 minute. Roll into a ball and flatten top to form a loaf about 9 inches in diameter. With a floured butter knife or spatula, cut top of dough about ¼ inch deep into equal sections (one cut north and south through the center, the other east and west through the center). Place on greased baking sheet, brush with melted butter, and bake 30 to 40 minutes.

Makes 1 loaf.

BEER AND CHEESE BREAD

Although self-rising flour is generally not recommended for use in bread, it works beautifully in this quick bread recipe.

3½ cups self-rising flour
2½ tablespoons sugar
1 can (12 ounces) warm beer

½ cup grated cheddar cheese
   (4 ounces)
½ cup melted butter (1 stick)

Preheat oven to 350°. Mix together all but last ingredient. Pour into lightly greased 9-inch loaf pan, pour melted butter over top, and bake 1 hour, or until done.

Makes 1 loaf.

CARAWAY BREAD

A spicy, fragrant loaf.

½ cup milk
6 tablespoons butter
2 cups flour
2 teaspoons baking powder
¼ teaspoon freshly grated
    nutmeg

½ teaspoon salt
1 cup sugar
3 tablespoons caraway seed
2 tablespoons chopped
    candied lemon peel
2 eggs

Preheat oven to 350°. Scald milk, add butter, and stir until butter melts. Set aside to cool. Sift together dry ingredients and stir in caraway seed and lemon peel. In bread bowl beat eggs into milk and butter. Add sifted ingredients and mix well. Bake in greased 7-inch loaf pan 50 to 60 minutes. *Makes 1 loaf.*

ORANGE-CARAWAY BREAD

Use freshly squeezed orange juice for this tasty bread.

2 cups flour
2 teaspoons baking powder
½ teaspoon salt
4 tablespoons butter
    (½ stick)
1 egg

¼ cup grated orange peel
2 tablespoons caraway seed
½ cup orange juice
¾ cup milk
½ cup sugar

Preheat oven to 350°. Sift together flour, baking powder, and salt. Cut in butter until mixture is crumbly. Combine egg, orange peel, caraway seed, orange juice, milk, and sugar. Blend into dry ingredients. Pour into greased 8-inch loaf pan and bake 50 to 60 minutes. *Makes 1 loaf.*

BRAN BREAD

A good-sized loaf for tea sandwiches.

3 cups flour
¼ cup sugar
2 teaspoons baking soda
¼ teaspoon salt
4 cups bran cereal

1½ cups raisins or currants
2 eggs
3 tablespoons melted butter
1½ cups milk
1 cup dark molasses

Preheat oven to 325°. Sift together flour, sugar, soda, and salt. Stir in bran and raisins. Beat together eggs, butter, milk, and molasses. Add to dry ingredients and stir until mixed. (Add more milk if necessary to form a thin batter.) Pour into 2 greased 9-inch loaf pans and bake 50 to 60 minutes. When done, bread will fill pans about ⅔ full.

Makes 2 loaves.

GRANDMA'S BRAN BREAD

A rich bread, good warm or cold.

1½ cups flour
½ teaspoon salt
1½ teaspoons baking powder
1½ teaspoons baking soda
1½ cups buttermilk
1 cup peach or strawberry jam

1 egg
1½ cups bran cereal
⅓ cup cornmeal
½ cup chopped dates, raisins,
    or currants

Preheat oven to 350°. Sift together flour, salt, baking powder, and soda. Beat together buttermilk, jam, and egg. Add sifted ingredients along with bran and cornmeal. Stir in dates. Bake in greased 9-inch loaf pan 40 to 50 minutes. *Makes 1 loaf.*

CHEESE AND BRAN BREAD

A great beginning for BLT's.

1½ cups flour	½ cup brown sugar
½ teaspoon baking soda	1 egg
1 teaspoon baking powder	1 cup buttermilk
¼ teaspoon salt	1 cup grated cheddar cheese
3 tablespoons butter	1 cup bran cereal

Preheat oven to 350°. Sift together flour, soda, baking powder, and salt. Cream butter and brown sugar, and beat in egg and buttermilk. Add dry ingredients and mix until smooth. Stir in cheese and bran. Bake in greased 9-inch loaf pan 50 to 60 minutes.   *Makes 1 loaf.*

GRAHAM BREAD

Add raisins to make a tea loaf.

2 teaspoons baking soda	⅔ cup molasses
¼ cup water	½ teaspoon salt
2½ cups buttermilk	4 cups graham flour
½ cup brown sugar	½ cup raisins (optional)

Preheat oven to 375°. In large bowl dissolve soda in water and stir in buttermilk. Add brown sugar, molasses, and salt. Beat in flour, 1 cup at a time, to form a soft dough. Add raisins, if used. Pour into 2 greased 8-inch loaf pans and bake 50 to 60 minutes.

Makes 2 loaves.

GRAHAM NUT BREAD

Delightful for lunch with cheese and apples, or toasted for breakfast.

2 cups flour	¾ cup raisins
4 teaspoons baking powder	2 eggs, beaten
1 teaspoon salt	1⅔ cups milk
¾ cup sugar	4 tablespoons melted butter
2 cups graham flour	(½ stick)
¾ cup chopped nuts	

Preheat oven to 350°. Sift together flour, baking powder, salt, and sugar. Add graham flour, nuts, and raisins. Combine eggs, milk, and butter; add to dry ingredients and blend. Bake in 2 greased 7-inch loaf pans 50 to 60 minutes. Remove from pans and cool on racks. Store overnight before slicing.   *Makes 2 loaves.*

GRAPE-NUTS BREAD

Hefty texture and nutty flavor; good hot or toasted for breakfast or brunch.

1 cup Grape-nuts cereal
1 cup milk
½ cup sugar
1 egg

1¾ cups flour
3 heaping teaspoons baking powder

Preheat oven to 325°. Combine Grape-nuts and milk in bowl and let stand 5 to 10 minutes. Cream sugar and egg until light. Stir in cereal mixture. Sift together flour and baking powder, and stir into cereal. Pour into greased 8-inch loaf pan and let stand 5 minutes. Bake for 40 to 50 minutes, until bread tests done. Turn out and cool on rack.

Makes 1 loaf.

ALMOND BREAD

A special treat to have with Thanksgiving dinner.

6 tablespoons butter
⅔ cup sugar
2 teaspoons almond extract
2 eggs

1½ cups flour
2 teaspoons baking powder
½ teaspoon salt
½ cup thinly sliced almonds

Preheat oven to 350°. Cream butter and sugar. Beat in almond extract and eggs. Sift together dry ingredients and beat into butter mixture. Fold in almonds. Bake in greased 9-inch loaf pan 50 to 60 minutes.

Makes 1 loaf.

LEMON NUT BREAD

Slice thin and enjoy any time.

4 tablespoons butter (½ stick)	2 teaspoons baking powder
½ cup sugar	½ teaspoon salt
2 eggs	¾ cup milk
1 tablespoon grated lemon rind	1 cup chopped nuts
2 cups flour	3 teaspoons lemon juice
	2 tablespoons sugar

Preheat oven to 350°. Cream butter and ½ cup sugar. Beat in eggs and lemon rind. Sift together flour, baking powder, and salt. Beat dry ingredients, ½ cup at a time, into butter and egg mixture, alternately adding milk. Beat until smooth. Stir in nuts. Pour into greased 9-inch loaf pan and bake 50 to 60 minutes. Cool in pan and remove to rack. Combine lemon juice and 2 tablespoons sugar in saucepan, bring to boil, cool, and pour over top of bread. (Place wax paper under bread to catch excess glaze.) Let sit several hours or overnight before cutting. *Makes 1 loaf.*

PEANUT BUTTER BREAD

Use creamy or crunchy peanut butter with equally pleasing results.

2 cups flour	⅓ cup sugar
4 teaspoons baking powder	½ cup peanut butter
½ teaspoon salt	1½ cups milk

Preheat oven to 350°. Sift together flour, baking powder, salt, and sugar. Add peanut butter and mix well. Add milk and blend until smooth. Bake in greased 8-inch loaf pan 50 to 60 minutes. Let sit 5 minutes and turn out onto rack to cool. *Makes 1 loaf.*

WALNUT BREAD

Take care not to overbeat the batter.

2 cups flour
5 tablespoons sugar
1 tablespoon baking powder
½ teaspoon salt
1 teaspoon freshly grated
    nutmeg

1 cup finely chopped walnuts
1 egg
1 cup milk
2 tablespoons melted butter

Preheat oven to 375°. Sift together dry ingredients. Add nuts. Beat together egg and milk, and add to dry ingredients along with butter. Blend quickly, just enough to moisten evenly. Pour into greased 9-inch loaf pan and bake 30 to 40 minutes.   *Makes 1 loaf.*

IV.
Breakfast
Pastries

APPLE PIE

A New England breakfast special.

7 to 8 tart apples, peeled,
    cored, and thinly sliced
½ cup brown or white sugar
½ teaspoon cinnamon
½ teaspoon salt
1 tablespoon lemon juice
Butter

Preheat oven to 450°. Prepare pastry for 2-crust pie (see page 84), and fit bottom pie crust into 9-inch pie plate. Arrange apples in rows along bottom and in layers, making the highest point in the center. Stir together sugar, cinnamon, salt, and lemon juice, and distribute over apples. Dot with butter. Moisten edges on bottom crust with cold water, cover with top crust, and press edges together. Slash or prick holes in top crust for steam to escape and bake 10 minutes. Reduce heat to 350° and bake 30 to 40 minutes longer.

Makes one 9-inch pie.

PRUNE PIE

Serve for brunch along with scrambled eggs and sausages.

1 pound pitted prunes
1 cup water
½ cup brown sugar
1 lemon
Butter
1 tablespoon flour

Preheat oven to 450°. Prepare pastry for 2-crust pie (see page 84). Combine prunes, water, and brown sugar in saucepan. Cut lemon into halves and juice. Add juice and halves to prune mixture, bring to a boil, reduce heat, and simmer 15 minutes. Line an 8-inch pie plate with pastry for bottom crust. Remove prunes from saucepan with slotted spoon and fill bottom crust. Discard lemon, bring remaining liquid to a boil, and cook over medium-high heat until thickened and reduced to several tablespoons. Pour over prunes, dot with butter, sprinkle with flour, add top crust, cut slits, and bake 10 minutes. Reduce heat to 350° and make 30 to 40 minutes longer.

Makes one 8-inch pie.

PIE CRUST

This recipe requires a quick hand and a light touch.

2 cups flour
1 teaspoon salt

⅔ cup shortening or lard
⅓ cup cold water

Sift together flour and salt. Cut in shortening until mixture is crumbly. Mix in water, stirring quickly with a fork until dough can be gathered into a ball. (If more water is necessary, add drop by drop.) Work quickly and handle dough as little as possible. Divide in half, wrap each in wax paper, flatten slightly, and chill several hours before rolling out on floured board.   *Makes 2 crusts for 9-inch pie.*

TURNOVERS

Good for breakfast as well as dessert.

Make pastry as for pie crust (see preceding recipe). Roll out dough and cut into 4- to 5-inch squares or circles. Place 1 to 2 tablespoons jam or fruit pie filling in the center of each, moisten edges with cold water, fold edges over, and press together with a fork to seal. Prick tops in several places and bake on greased baking sheets in preheated 450° oven 12 to 15 minutes.   *Makes 1 dozen.*

CROISSANTS

Although not New England in origin, these flaky pastries are a sublime breakfast treat. Practice makes perfect, so keep trying if your first attempt doesn't measure up to your expectations. One of the secrets is to prevent the dough from rising prior to baking.

2 packages dry yeast
2 teaspoons sugar
1½ teaspoons salt
3½ cups flour
12 ounces butter (in one block)

¾ cup cold milk
3 egg yolks
1 tablespoon cream

Combine yeast, sugar, salt, and flour. Cut in 2 tablespoons (1 ounce) butter and add milk to form a semi-stiff dough. (Dough should not be sticky — add a bit more flour or milk if necessary.) Turn out onto floured board and knead briefly until smooth. (Don't go as far as you would in making bread dough.) Refrigerate 15 minutes. Place remaining butter between 2 sheets of wax paper and roll out to ¼-inch thickness. Cut in half the long way and refrigerate. When dough has chilled, roll it out on a floured board into a rectangle about ¼ inch thick. Visually divide rectangle into thirds. Place ½ of chilled butter in center, and fold left-hand side over to cover butter. Place other piece of butter on top of this fold and bring right-hand side over to cover this piece. Roll dough out into ¼-inch-thick rectangle again. Now visually divide dough into quarters; fold over the left- and right-hand quarters. Then fold again. (Dough will resemble a closed book jacket.) Press edges together. Wrap in wax paper and chill 2 hours. Unwrap and place on lightly floured board. Roll out and repeat folding as in latter procedure. Wrap and chill 3 to 4 hours. Cut dough into 2 equal parts and roll out very thin. Cut into strips 6 inches wide. Cut strips into triangles and loosely roll up base (widest side) toward point. Place on greased baking sheets and chill 2 hours. Remove 2 at a time and roll gently to form into longer, tighter rolls. Curve slightly, and return to refrigerator for 2 hours. Preheat oven to 475°. Beat together egg yolks and cream and brush mixture on top of each roll. Bake 5 minutes; reduce heat to 400°, and bake 8 to 10 minutes longer or until golden.   *Makes 30-34.*

BREAKFAST RING

A wonderful treat for overnight guests.

1 package dry yeast
¼ cup warm water
½ cup milk
2 tablespoons butter
3 tablespoons sugar
¼ teaspoon salt

· 1 egg
2 to 3 cups flour
2 tablespoons softened butter
½ cup strawberry, blackberry,
   apricot, or peach jam
½ cup chopped pecans

Dissolve yeast in warm water and set aside. Scald milk, add butter, remove from heat, and stir until butter melts. Add sugar and salt. When cool, combine with yeast. Beat in egg and flour, 1 cup at a time, to form a soft dough. Turn out onto floured board and knead, adding more flour as necessary to form a smooth dough. Place dough in buttered bowl, turn to grease top, cover, and let rise until doubled. Punch down. Roll out into rectangle ¼ inch thick and about 20 inches long. Spread with butter and jam. Sprinkle with nuts. Roll up in a tight jelly roll, beginning at the long end. Finish with seam on the bottom. Shape into a ring and pinch the ends to seal. Use scissors to cut across top of ring every few inches making wedge-shaped cuts into top layer of dough. Fold cut edges over to expose filling inside. Cover and let rise until doubled. Bake in preheated 350° oven 20 to 30 minutes.   *Makes 1 ring.*

BLUEBERRY COFFEE CAKE

Use wild blueberries if you can find them.

1 package dry yeast	½ teaspoon salt
¼ cup warm water	½ cup brown sugar
1 cup milk	1 cup blueberries
4 tablespoons butter (½ stick)	Melted butter
1 egg, beaten	¼ cup sugar
3 to 4 cups flour	2 teaspoons cinnamon

Dissolve yeast in warm water and set aside. Scald milk and stir in butter until melted. When cool, beat in egg. Sift together flour and salt. Combine yeast, milk and egg mixture, and brown sugar, and beat in flour, 1 cup at a time, to form a stiff dough. Turn out onto floured board and knead until smooth. Shape into a ball, place in buttered bowl, turn to grease top, cover, and let rise until doubled. Turn out onto floured board, gently knead in blueberries, and roll out into a rope. Shape into a ring and place in greased 1½-quart ring mold or tube pan; pinch ends together. Cover and let rise until doubled. Bake in preheated 375° oven 25 to 30 minutes. Invert and brush with melted butter. Combine ¼ cup sugar with cinnamon and sprinkle on top and sides. *Makes 1 ring.*

BLUEBERRY-SOUR CREAM COFFEE CAKE

A delectable way to use that last handful of blueberries.

2 cups flour	1½ cups sugar
2 teaspoons baking powder	1 cup sour cream
½ teaspoon salt	½ cup blueberries
1 cup softened butter (2 sticks)	3 tablespoons sugar
2 eggs	1 teaspoon cinnamon
1 teaspoon vanilla	1 teaspoon lemon juice

Preheat oven to 350°. Sift together flour, baking powder, and salt. Cream butter, eggs, vanilla, and 1½ cups sugar. Fold in sour cream. Beat in sifted ingredients to form a smooth batter. In separate bowl combine berries, 3 tablespoons sugar, cinnamon, and lemon juice. Spoon half the batter into greased 9-inch round pan. Cover with filling and pour in rest of batter. Bake 50 to 60 minutes. Frost with White Icing (see page 134). *Makes one 9-inch cake.*

CRANBERRY SWIRL COFFEE CAKE

For a cherry-like flavor, substitute almond extract for the vanilla and top with Almond Icing.

½ cup softened butter (1 stick)
1 cup sugar
2 eggs
2 cups flour
1 teaspoon baking powder
1 teaspoon baking soda
½ teaspoon salt
1 cup yogurt
1 teaspoon vanilla
1 can (16 ounces) whole
   cranberry sauce
½ cup chopped nuts

Preheat oven to 375°. Cream butter, then gradually add sugar and blend until fluffy. Add eggs, 1 at a time, beating after each addition. Sift together dry ingredients and add to batter alternately with yogurt. Add vanilla. Grease a tube pan and spread a thin layer of batter over the bottom. Stir the cranberry sauce so it is well mixed, then spread a thin layer of it over the batter. Add another layer of batter, a layer of cranberry sauce, a layer of batter, and end with cranberry sauce. Sprinkle nuts over top, then bake for 55 minutes, or until toothpick inserted into cake comes out clean. Cool in pan on rack for 5 minutes. Remove from pan and dribble Almond or White Icing (see p. 134) over the top. *Makes 1 cake.*

CURRANT COFFEE CAKE

Best served hot from the oven with lots of butter.

2 cups flour
2 teaspoons baking powder
½ teaspoon salt
1 cup sugar
1 teaspoon cinnamon
6 tablespoons butter
1 egg, beaten
1 cup milk
½ cup currants
1½ tablespoons melted butter
4 tablespoons sugar
1 tablespoon flour
½ teaspoon cinnamon

Preheat oven to 400°. Sift together flour, baking powder, salt, 1 cup sugar, and 1 teaspoon cinnamon. Cut in butter. Combine egg and milk, and add to flour mixture, stirring gently. Add currants and stir until blended. Turn into greased 9-inch round cake pan, and spread dough evenly. Brush top with melted butter. Mix together 4 tablespoons sugar, flour, and ½ teaspoon cinnamon, and sift evenly over top of dough. Bake 25 to 30 minutes. *Makes one 9-inch cake.*

SOUR CREAM COFFEE CAKE

Easy to make, and perfect for a special breakfast.

½ cup softened butter (1 stick)
1 cup white sugar
2 eggs
1 cup sour cream
1 teaspoon vanilla
2 cups flour

1 teaspoon baking powder
1 teaspoon baking soda
¼ teaspoon salt
½ cup chopped walnuts
1 teaspoon cinnamon
⅓ cup light brown sugar

Preheat oven to 350°. Cream butter and white sugar. Beat in eggs, and add sour cream and vanilla. Sift together dry ingredients and add, stirring to form a smooth batter. Put half the batter in greased and floured 1½-quart tube pan. Combine walnuts, cinnamon, and brown sugar, and sprinkle half of this mixture over batter. Add remaining batter and sprinkle remaining topping over it. Bake 35 to 45 minutes. *Makes 1 ring.*

CHERRY SWEET ROLLS

Substitute raisins, nuts, currants, or fresh chopped citrus rind to flavor the filling and frosting.

1 package dry yeast
¼ cup warm water
1 cup milk
4 tablespoons butter (½ stick)
1 egg
⅓ cup sugar
½ teaspoon salt

2½ cups flour
4 tablespoons melted butter
2 tablespoons milk
1 tablespoon finely chopped
    maraschino cherries
1 to 1½ cups powdered sugar

Dissolve yeast in warm water. Scald 1 cup milk and stir in butter until melted. When cool, beat in egg, sugar, and salt. Add to yeast mixture and blend in flour to form a sticky dough. Cover and let rise until doubled. Punch down and roll out onto well-floured board, forming a rectangle ½ inch thick. Combine melted butter, 2 tablespoons milk, cherries, and powdered sugar. Spread ¾ of mixture onto dough. Roll dough up and cut into ½-inch slices. Place on greased baking sheet, cover, and let rise until doubled. Bake in preheated 350° oven 20 to 30 minutes. When cool, frost with remaining filling. *Makes 2 dozen.*

CINNAMON ROLLS

Make these rolls to feed a hungry breakfast crowd.

2 packages dry yeast
¼ cup warm water
2 cups milk
4 tablespoons butter (½ stick)
3 eggs
½ cup sugar
4 to 6 cups flour

1 teaspoon salt
1 teaspoon cinnamon
4 tablespoons softened butter
3 teaspoons cinnamon
5 tablespoons sugar
1 egg white
2 tablespoons milk

Dissolve yeast in warm water and set aside. Scald milk and stir in butter until melted. Cool and beat in eggs. Sift together ½ cup sugar, 4 cups flour, salt, and 1 teaspoon cinnamon. Blend in milk and yeast mixtures. Add more flour as necessary to form a firm dough. Turn out onto floured board and knead until smooth. Place in buttered bowl, turn to grease top, cover, and let rise until doubled. Punch down, divide in half, and roll both pieces out to ¼-inch thickness. Spread each half with softened butter; mix together 3 teaspoons cinnamon and 5 tablespoons sugar, and sprinkle over butter. Roll up into jelly roll, and cut into ¼-inch slices. Place on greased baking sheet. Cover and let rise until doubled. Bake in preheated 350° oven 20 minutes. When cooled, frost with White Icing (see page 134); or, after removing from oven, brush with egg white and milk, and return to oven several minutes to brown. *Makes 4 dozen.*

CINNAMON CURRANT ROLLS

A favorite with children.

2½ cups flour
2 teaspoons baking powder
¼ teaspoon salt
4 tablespoons butter (½ stick)
¾ cup milk
2 tablespoons softened butter

½ cup brown sugar
1 teaspoon cinnamon
½ cup currants or chopped
  nuts
4 tablespoons melted butter
4 tablespoons brown sugar

Preheat oven to 425°. Sift together flour, baking powder, and salt. Cut in 4 tablespoons butter until mixture is crumbly. Pour in milk and stir quickly to form a soft dough. Turn out onto floured board and knead several times. Roll out to ¼-inch thickness. Mix together softened butter, ½ cup brown sugar, and cinnamon. Spread on dough and sprinkle with currants. Roll dough up into jelly roll and cut into 1-inch slices. Measure 1 teaspoon melted butter into each of 12 large muffin pan sections. Add 1 teaspoon brown sugar to each section. Place rolls in pans, flat sides down, and bake 15 minutes. Reduce heat to 350° and bake 10 to 15 minutes longer. Remove from pans to cool.   *Makes 1 dozen.*

PECAN ROLLS

Sweet and irresistible.

2 packages dry yeast	5 to 6 cups flour
½ cup warm water	5 tablespoons butter
⅔ cup milk	1 cup brown sugar
½ cup butter (1 stick)	1 cup chopped pecans
⅓ cup white sugar	¼ cup maple syrup
1 teaspoon salt	2 tablespoons softened butter
2 eggs	½ cup brown sugar

Dissolve yeast in warm water and set aside. Scald milk, add ½ cup butter, white sugar, and salt, and stir until butter melts. When cool, beat in eggs. Add flour, 1 cup at a time, to form a stiff dough. Turn out onto floured board and knead until smooth. Shape into a ball, place in buttered bowl, turn to grease top, cover, and let rise until doubled.

When bread has doubled, melt 5 tablespoons butter in saucepan, stir in 1 cup brown sugar, pecans, and maple syrup. Bring just to a boil, reduce heat, and simmer 5 minutes, stirring to prevent sticking. Set aside.

Punch down risen dough, divide in half, and roll both pieces out into rectangle ½ inch thick. Spread each with 1 tablespoon softened butter, sprinkle each with ¼ cup brown sugar, and roll up, starting at the longest edge. Pinch seams to seal. Cut into 1-inch slices. Pour 1 tablespoon brown sugar and pecan sauce into each section of greased muffin pans. Place a slice of dough in each section. Cover and let rise until doubled. Bake in preheated 400° oven 20 to 25 minutes. Turn pans upside down and tap bottoms to remove rolls.
                                        Makes about 2 dozen.

RAISIN COFFEE ROLLS

A welcome change from toast for breakfast.

3 cups flour
1 tablespoon baking powder
½ teaspoon salt
2 tablespoons white sugar
6 tablespoons butter
¾ cup milk

2 tablespoons softened butter
2 tablespoons brown sugar
½ cup raisins
1 egg yolk, beaten
2 tablespoons white sugar
¼ cup chopped pecans

Preheat oven to 425°. Sift together flour, baking powder, salt, and 2 tablespoons white sugar. Cut in butter until mixture is crumbly. Add milk and stir quickly to form a soft dough. Turn out onto floured board and knead several times. Roll out ¼ inch thick and cut into 3-inch squares. Spread with softened butter, and sprinkle with brown sugar and raisins. Roll each square up jelly-roll style. Brush with egg yolk, dust with white sugar, and sprinkle with nuts. Place on ungreased baking sheet and bake 10 to 15 minutes.

Makes 2 dozen.

SCONES

An easy breakfast pastry that everyone likes.

2 cups flour
4 teaspoons baking powder
½ teaspoon salt
2 teaspoons sugar

4 tablespoons butter (½ stick)
2 eggs
¾ cup cream

Preheat oven to 425°. Sift together flour, baking powder, salt, and sugar. Cut in butter until mixture is crumbly. Beat together eggs and cream, and add to dry ingredients, stirring with a fork until just moistened. Divide dough in half and gently pat into 2 greased 8-inch cake pans. Cut into quarters and bake 15 to 20 minutes.   *Makes 8.*

RAISIN SCONES

Sure to please any breakfast guest.

2 cups flour
1 tablespoon sugar
½ teaspoon salt
1 tablespoon baking powder

½ cup butter (1 stick)
½ cup raisins or currants
1 egg, beaten
½ to ¾ cup milk

Preheat oven to 425°. Sift together flour, sugar, salt, and baking powder. Cut in butter until mixture is crumbly. Stir in raisins. Blend in egg and milk to form a soft dough. Turn out onto floured board and knead gently until smooth. Divide in two and shape each half into a ball. Roll out to ½-inch thickness. Cut each circle into 8 wedge-shaped pieces. Place on greased baking sheet (if desired, brush with a beaten egg) and bake 10 to 12 minutes until brown.

Makes 16.

SOUR CREAM SCONES

Make your own sour cream to use in this recipe.

2 cups flour
3 tablespoons sugar
2 teaspoons baking powder
½ teaspoon baking soda
½ teaspoon salt

⅓ cup butter
2 teaspoons vinegar
⅔ cup all-purpose whipping
   cream
1 egg yolk

Preheat oven to 425°. Sift together dry ingredients. Cut in butter until mixture is crumbly. Stir vinegar into cream. Beat in egg yolk and add mixture to dry ingredients to form a soft dough. Roll out onto floured board to ½-inch thickness and cut into 2-inch biscuits. Place on greased baking sheet and bake 10 to 12 minutes.

Makes 2 dozen.

ENGLISH MUFFINS

Cook in a cast-iron skillet, not quite as hot as the one required for pancakes.

1 package dry yeast	3 tablespoons sugar
1 cup warm water	1 teaspoon salt
1 cup milk	5 to 6 cups flour
4 tablespoons butter (½ stick)	Cornmeal

Dissolve yeast in warm water and set aside. Scald milk, add butter, sugar, and salt, and stir until butter melts. Cool and add to yeast. Beat in flour, 1 cup at a time, to form a soft dough. Knead gently in bowl, and shape into a ball. Place in buttered bowl, turn to grease top, cover, and let rise until doubled. Punch down and divide into 2 pieces. Gently pat or roll both out to ½-inch thickness on board sprinkled with cornmeal. Cut into 3- to 3½-inch circles with the rim of a glass. Place on ungreased baking sheets 3 inches apart and let rise until doubled. Grease and heat cast-iron skillet and cook each muffin, starting with cornmeal side, 10 to 12 minutes per side until puffy and brown. Cool on racks. *Makes 14-20.*

BAGELS

Serve with cream cheese.

1 cup milk	3 eggs
2 teaspoons sugar	4 to 5 cups flour
4 tablespoons butter (½ stick)	2 quarts water
2 teaspoons salt	4 tablespoons sugar
1 package dry yeast	1 egg white, beaten slightly

Scald milk, add 2 teaspoons sugar, butter, and salt. Stir until butter melts. Cool, then add yeast, stir until dissolved, and set aside 10 minutes. Beat in eggs and flour, 1 cup at a time, to form a soft dough. Turn out onto floured board and knead, blending in more flour as necessary until dough is smooth. Shape into a ball, place in buttered bowl, turn to grease top, cover, and let rise until doubled. Punch down and roll out into a rectangle ½ to ¼ inch thick. Cut into 20 equal strips and roll each into a rope, tapering at the ends. Wrap around your thumb into a ring shape, leaving a hole a little larger than a quarter. Tuck the ends under. Place on floured baking sheet, cover, and let rise 30 minutes. Bring water and 4 tablespoons sugar to a boil in pot, reduce heat to a simmer, and drop in bagels, 2 or 3 at a time. Cook for about 4 minutes, or until they swell. Remove with slotted spoon, drain, and place on ungreased baking sheet. Brush with egg white. Bake in preheated 400° oven 25 to 30 minutes or until brown. *Makes 20.*

For Onion Bagels: Mince 2 onions and fry in 1 tablespoon oil until crisp. Drain well. Add to dough, mix well, knead, and proceed as directed above. If desired, reserve a bit of onion and gently press into egg wash before baking.

For Cinnamon-Raisin Bagels: Add 1 cup raisins and 1 teaspoon cinnamon to dough. Mix well, knead, and proceed with recipe.

BAKED DOUGHNUTS

For those who can't eat fried foods.

1 package dry yeast
¼ cup warm water
1½ cups milk
⅓ cup butter
5 cups flour
1 teaspoon salt

¼ cup sugar
½ teaspoon nutmeg
½ teaspoon ginger
2 eggs
Melted butter

Dissolve yeast in warm water and set aside. Scald milk, add butter, and stir until butter melts. Sift together flour, salt, sugar, nutmeg, and ginger. Pour milk mixture into bread bowl and when cool, beat in eggs. Add yeast and beat in dry ingredients to form a soft dough. Cover and let rise until doubled. Punch down, turn out onto floured board, and knead several times. Roll out to ½-inch thickness and cut with doughnut cutter. Place several inches apart on greased baking sheets, and let rise until doubled. Brush with melted butter and bake in preheated 425° oven 10 to 12 minutes. If desired, sprinkle with sugar. *Makes 3 dozen.*

RAISED DOUGHNUTS

These will keep fresh for several days if they are stored in a tightly sealed plastic bag.

1 package dry yeast
½ cup warm water
½ cup warm milk
½ cup butter (1 stick)
½ cup sugar

2 eggs
2 teaspoons vanilla
1 teaspoon salt
6 to 7 cups flour

Dissolve yeast in warm water and set aside. Scald milk, add butter and sugar, and stir until butter melts. When cool, combine milk mixture with yeast, eggs, vanilla, and salt. Beat in flour, 1 cup at a time, to form a soft dough. Cover and let rise until doubled. Roll out ½ inch thick and cut with doughnut cutter. Place doughnuts on greased baking sheet, cover, and let rise 30 minutes. Fry in hot oil until golden. If desired, glaze with a mixture of 1 cup powdered sugar and 1 tablespoon vanilla.   *Makes 24-30.*

BANANA DOUGHNUTS

An enticingly unusual recipe.

4 cups flour
4 teaspoons baking powder
1 teaspoon baking soda
2 teaspoons salt
1 teaspoon nutmeg
4 tablespoons butter (½ stick)

1 cup sugar
3 eggs, well beaten
1½ teaspoons vanilla
¾ cup mashed bananas
½ cup sour milk

Sift together flour, baking powder, soda, salt, and nutmeg. Cream butter and gradually beat in sugar until mixture is fluffy. Beat in eggs. Combine vanilla, bananas, and sour milk, and beat into creamed mixture. Add flour mixture and blend until smooth. Taking a small amount of dough at a time, knead briefly on lightly floured board and roll out ¾ inch thick. Cut into doughnuts. Fry in deep fat (heated to 375°) for 3 to 5 minutes, until golden brown. Drain, and sprinkle with sugar if desired.   *Makes 2 dozen.*

BLUEBERRY DOUGHNUTS

The berries add a subtle flavor and color.

2 cups flour
2 teaspoons baking powder

2 eggs
4 tablespoons melted butter
ick)
lueberries

Si
m
bl
in
br

salt. Beat together
edients. Fold in
d, and roll out ¼ to ½
h hot fat, turning to
Makes 2 dozen.

C

UTS I

oons vanilla
oon baking soda
ups flour
spoon baking powder
oon salt

and vanilla. Sift
nd salt. Beat into
adding more flour if
. Roll out on floured
ut cutter and fry in hot
ar or spread with White
Makes 3 dozen.

BUTTERMILK DOUGHNUTS II

Split leftovers, spread with butter, and place under broiler to toast.

1 cup sugar
2 eggs
½ teaspoon salt
1 tablespoon baking powder
1 teaspoon baking soda
½ teaspoon freshly grated
    nutmeg

½ teaspoon cinnamon
1 cup buttermilk
2 tablespoons melted butter
4 cups flour

Beat together all ingredients except flour to form a smooth batter. Beat in flour, 1 cup at a time, to form a soft dough. Roll out onto floured board to ¼-inch thickness. Cut with doughnut cutter and fry in hot fat until golden. *Makes 3 dozen.*

POTATO DOUGHNUTS

Best served while still warm; these doughnuts do not keep well.

1 cup mashed potatoes
½ cup brown sugar
1½ cups milk
2 eggs, beaten

3 to 4 cups flour
2 teaspoons baking powder
½ teaspoon salt
½ teaspoon cinnamon

Beat together potatoes, brown sugar, milk, and eggs. Sift together 3 cups flour, baking powder, salt, and cinnamon, and add to potato mixture. If necessary add more flour to form a stiff dough. Roll out to ½-inch thickness and cut with doughnut cutter. Fry in 370° fat until brown. Drain on paper towels. If desired, sprinkle with a mixture of sugar and cinnamon. *Makes 2½ dozen.*

SQUASH DOUGHNUTS

Tasty doughnuts with a light yellow color.

1½ cups sugar
⅔ cup cooked, mashed winter
   squash (acorn, butternut,
   Hubbard)
2 eggs
1 tablespoon butter
1 cup buttermilk

1 teaspoon vanilla
1½ teaspoons baking soda
2 teaspoons baking powder
½ teaspoon salt
½ teaspoon nutmeg
½ teaspoon ginger
3 cups flour

Beat together sugar, squash, eggs, butter, buttermilk, and vanilla. Sift together remaining ingredients and beat into egg and squash mixture to form a soft dough. Roll out on floured board until ¼ to ½ inch thick. Cut with doughnut cutter and fry in hot fat, turning so both sides are brown. *Makes 3 dozen.*

CRULLERS

Make as twisted rods or shape into rings.

3 tablespoons softened butter
1 cup sugar
3 eggs
1 cup all-purpose whipping
   cream

4 cups flour
1 tablespoon baking powder
¼ teaspoon nutmeg
1 teaspoon salt

Cream butter and sugar. Beat in eggs and cream. Sift together flour, baking powder, nutmeg, and salt, and add to wet ingredients, beating to form a smooth dough. Turn out onto floured board and knead gently. Pat out to ½-inch thickness, cut into strips ¼ inch wide and 6 to 8 inches long. Braid several strips together. Shape into rods and pinch ends together, or make into rings and fold ends under. Fry in hot fat until golden. Drain on paper towels and dust with sugar. *Makes 1-2 dozen.*

INDIAN BREAD

An unusual bread, based on a very old recipe, that is easy to make. Children love it.

1 cup milk	1 teaspoon cinnamon
1 tablespoon butter	1 tablespoon baking powder
2½ cups flour	2 tablespoons oil
1 teaspoon salt	

Scald milk, add butter, and stir until melted. Set aside to cool. Sift together flour, salt, cinnamon, and baking powder. Slowly beat milk and butter into dry ingredients. Turn mixture out onto floured board and knead gently until smooth. Divide dough into 2 equal pieces and roll each out as thin as you can on floured board. Cut into pieces about 3 inches square. Heat oil in heavy skillet and fry dough quickly, turning when it is puffy and brown. (It will resemble pita bread.) Serve hot, sprinkled with a mixture of cinnamon and sugar.

Makes 20 to 24 pieces.

Filled Indian Bread: After rolling dough out very thin, cut into 4-inch squares. In the center of each, place a teaspoonful of jam, currants, or chopped raisins, or a thin slice of apple; fold over to form a triangle, turn up bottom edge, and pinch to seal. Fry as above.

CORN FRITTERS

Great with maple syrup. Don't underestimate how many you or your guests might eat!

1 cup canned corn, drained	½ teaspoon salt
⅔ cup flour	1 egg, separated
½ teaspoon baking powder	

Combine corn, flour, baking powder, and salt. Beat egg yolk and add. Beat egg white until stiff and fold in. Fry spoonfuls of mixture in hot fat until puffy and brown, about 5 minutes.   *Makes 2 dozen.*

FRUIT FRITTERS

Serve for brunch or dessert.

2 eggs, separated
⅔ cup milk
1 tablespoon melted butter
2 tablespoons sugar

1 cup flour
¼ teaspoon salt
Fruit for fritters (see below)

Beat egg yolks, and add milk and butter. Blend in sugar, flour, and salt, stirring gently until mixed. Beat egg whites until stiff and fold in. In heavy pan heat fat to 370°. Dust prepared fruit with flour, and with slotted spoon or sharp-tined fork dip each piece into batter, remove, allowing excess batter to drip back into bowl, and gently place in hot fat. Fry 3 to 5 minutes and drain on paper towels. Sprinkle with powdered sugar and serve.   *Serves 4-6.*

Apples: Use tart apples with good flavor. Peel, core, and slice.

Oranges: Peel, divide into sections, remove membranes and seeds, leaving skin intact.

Strawberries: Remove stem ends.

Plums and cherries: Remove pits, cut larger ones in halves.

PANCAKES

If you're feeding a crowd, keep pancakes warm in a 250° oven until you are ready to serve them.

2 cups flour
2 teaspoons baking powder
½ teaspoon salt
1 to 2 tablespoons sugar

2 eggs
3 tablespoons melted butter
2 cups milk (or more)

Sift together flour, baking powder, salt, and sugar. Beat together eggs, butter, and milk. Beat wet ingredients into dry to form a smooth batter. Spoon onto hot greased griddle or cast-iron frying pan. (Surface should be hot enough to sizzle when drops of water hit it.) When bubbles appear on top of the pancakes, turn and cook other side.   *Makes 2-3 dozen.*

APPLE PANCAKES

Use apples with a lot of flavor.

3 medium apples
1½ cups flour
1 teaspoon baking powder
2 tablespoons powdered sugar
½ teaspoon salt

3 eggs, separated
1½ cups milk
1 cup heavy cream
1 teaspoon vanilla

Peel apples, remove cores, and slice into paper-thin rings. Sift together flour, baking powder, powdered sugar, and salt. Beat in egg yolks, milk, cream, and vanilla. Beat egg whites until stiff and fold into batter. Drop batter in ¼-cup amounts onto hot griddle. Before bubbles form, push an apple ring or two into the top of each pancake. When bottom has browned, turn gently and brown other side. Serve with maple syrup or sprinkled with powdered sugar.

Makes 15-20.

BEER PANCAKES

Beer produces a unique flavor and texture.

1 to 1½ cups milk
1½ cups flour
2 eggs
2 teaspoons sugar

1 teaspoon salt
½ teaspoon vanilla
½ cup beer

Combine 1 cup milk with remaining ingredients and beat until smooth. (Add up to ½ cup more milk if necessary to form a thin batter.) Fry by spoonfuls on hot greased griddle. When bubbles form, turn and brown other side.

Makes 2-3 dozen.

CORN PANCAKES

Try these with two cups buttermilk for even more zip.

2 cups raw fresh corn
2 cups flour
2 teaspoons baking powder
½ teaspoon salt

1 tablespoon sugar
1 egg, beaten
1½ cups milk
2 tablespoons melted butter

Combine all ingredients in bowl and blend well. Spoon onto hot griddle, and when bubbles appear on the surface, turn to brown other side. Serve with butter and maple syrup.   *Serves 3-4.*

RAISED PANCAKES

These have more substance than regular pancakes.

1 package dry yeast
½ cup water
1½ cups milk
4 tablespoons butter (½ stick)
2 tablespoons sugar

1 teaspoon salt
½ teaspoon cinnamon
2 eggs, beaten
2 cups flour

Dissolve yeast in warm water. Scald milk, add butter, sugar, salt, and cinnamon, and stir until butter melts. Cool. Beat together yeast, milk mixture, and eggs. Add flour to form a thin batter. (If mixture runs off spoon in very thin stream, add a bit more flour.) Cover and let rise 30 minutes. (Do not stir down batter.) Fry by spoonfuls on hot griddle.   *Makes 2 dozen.*

WAFFLES

Be sure the waffle iron is hot before adding batter.

1½ cups flour
2 teaspoons baking powder
½ teaspoon salt
1 teaspoon sugar

3 eggs, separated
1¼ cups milk
5 tablespoons melted butter

Sift together dry ingredients. Beat egg yolks until light yellow, add milk and butter, and stir well. Add wet ingredients to dry, stirring quickly to form a smooth batter. Beat egg whites until stiff and fold into mixture. Pour 4 to 5 tablespoonfuls into center of hot waffle iron. Close lid and cook 3 to 5 minutes. (If there is no device to tell you when the iron is hot enough, add a spoonful of water to cold waffle iron, close, and heat; when no more steam appears, iron is hot enough for cooking waffles.) *Makes 6.*

Waffle Variations:

Add ½ cup grated cheese to batter.

Or, sprinkle batter with 1 tablespoon diced raw bacon before closing lid of iron.

Or, add ½ cup blueberries or ⅔ cup chopped, unpeeled apples to batter.

Or, add ½ cup cooked rice to batter.

APPLESAUCE WAFFLES

Serve with applesauce on the side.

2 cups flour
1 tablespoon baking powder
1 teaspoon salt
½ teaspoon cinnamon

½ cup applesauce
3 eggs, separated
1 cup milk
½ cup melted butter (1 stick)

Sift together flour, baking powder, salt, and cinnamon. Beat together applesauce, egg yolks, milk, and butter. Add wet ingredients to dry, stirring until smooth. Beat egg whites until stiff and fold in. Bake in hot waffle iron. *Makes 4-6.*

BUTTERMILK WAFFLES

Rich and flaky.

1 egg
1½ cups buttermilk
1½ cups flour
1 teaspoon baking soda

1 teaspoon baking powder
1 teaspoon salt
2 tablespoons melted butter

Beat egg until lemon colored. Add buttermilk and beat until blended. Sift together flour, soda, baking powder, and salt. Add to milk mixture and blend in butter to form a smooth batter. Bake in hot waffle iron.   *Makes 5-6.*

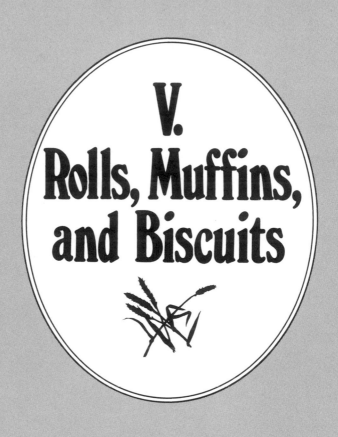

V.
Rolls, Muffins, and Biscuits

DINNER ROLLS

This dough can be shaped any way you wish.

2 packages dry yeast	½ cup melted butter (1 stick)
½ cup warm water	½ teaspoon salt
1 cup milk	1 egg, beaten
½ cup sugar	5 to 6 cups flour

Dissolve yeast in warm water and set aside. Scald milk, add sugar, butter, and salt, and stir until butter melts. Cool. Combine yeast and milk mixtures in bread bowl and blend in beaten egg. Beat in flour, 1 cup at a time, to form a stiff dough. Turn out onto floured board and knead until smooth. Place in buttered bowl, turn to grease top, cover, and let rise until doubled. Punch down and roll out into desired shapes (see pages 114-116). Place on greased baking sheets or in greased muffin pans. Cover and let rise until doubled. Bake in preheated 400° oven 15 to 20 minutes. *Makes 2-3 dozen.*

CREAM CHEESE ROLLS

Soft-textured rolls that enhance any meal.

1 package dry yeast	2 tablespoons honey
½ cup warm water	4 tablespoons softened cream
3 cups flour	cheese
½ teaspoon salt	3 tablespoons melted butter

Dissolve yeast in warm water and set aside. Sift together flour and salt. Cream honey, cream cheese, and butter. Add yeast to cream cheese mixture and blend. Add flour, 1 cup at a time, to form a soft dough. Turn out onto floured board and knead. (Dough will be sticky.) Place in buttered bowl, turn to grease top, cover, and let rise until doubled. Punch down, form into 8 round rolls, place on greased baking sheet, cover, and let rise until doubled. Bake in preheated 375° oven for 20 minutes or until golden. *Makes 8.*

KLARA'S ROLLS

These are versatile rolls that go with breakfast, lunch, or dinner.

1 package dry yeast	½ cup sugar
1 teaspoon sugar	1 teaspoon salt
1 tablespoon flour	1 lemon rind (whole lemon)
Pinch of salt	1 tablespoon butter
¼ cup warm milk	3 tablespoons sour cream
1 cup butter (2 sticks)	3 eggs
2 cups warm milk	1 egg, beaten
8 cups flour	Sesame or poppy seed

Mix together first 5 ingredients, cover, and let sit for 10 minutes. In separate bowl, combine butter and 2 cups milk, stirring until butter melts. In another bowl, mix flour, sugar, salt, and lemon rind. Add 1 tablespoon butter, sour cream, 3 eggs, butter and milk mixture, and stir to blend. Add yeast mixture and mix well. Knead on floured board about 5 minutes, until smooth and elastic; dough will be soft. Put in buttered bowl, turn to grease top, cover, and let rise for 2 hours. Roll out, divide into 30 balls, and shape like buns. Let rise about 1 hour. Brush tops with 1 beaten egg, sprinkle with sesame seed or poppy seed, and bake in preheated 350° oven for ½ hour.

Makes 2½ dozen.

PARSLEY ROLLS

Colorful rolls for lunch or dinner.

2 packages dry yeast	4 to 5 cups flour
½ cup warm water	½ teaspoon salt
¼ teaspoon sugar	2 to 3 tablespoons finely
1½ cups warm milk	chopped fresh parsley

Dissolve yeast in warm water, add sugar, and combine with milk. Sift together flour and salt, and gradually mix into wet ingredients. Turn onto floured board and knead until smooth. Place in buttered bowl, turn to grease top, cover, and let rise until doubled. Punch down, knead in parsley, and form into 24 small balls. Place on greased baking sheet, cover, and let rise 30 minutes. Bake in preheated 475° oven 8 to 10 minutes.

Makes 2 dozen.

POCKETBOOK ROLLS

These rolls freeze very well.

1 package dry yeast	3 to 4 cups flour
½ cup warm water	¼ cup sugar
1 cup milk	1 teaspoon salt
3 tablespoons butter	Melted butter
1 egg	

Dissolve yeast in warm water and set aside. Scald milk, add butter, and stir until melted. When cool, combine with yeast and beat in egg. Sift together 3 cups flour, sugar, and salt, and beat into wet ingredients, 1 cup at a time, to form a stiff dough. Add remaining flour as necessary. Turn out onto floured board and knead until smooth. Place in buttered bowl, turn to grease top, cover, and let rise until doubled. Punch down, knead, and roll out onto floured board to ½-inch thickness. Shape as desired (see pages 114-116). Place on greased baking sheet, cover, and let rise until doubled. Brush tops with melted butter. Bake in preheated 350° oven 15 to 20 minutes.

Makes 2-3 dozen.

REFRIGERATOR ROLLS

The dough for these light, all-purpose rolls can be mixed up ahead of time and refrigerated for two to three days.

2 packages dry yeast	2 eggs
½ cup warm water	¼ cup sugar
1 cup milk	1 teaspoon salt
½ cup butter (1 stick)	4 to 6 cups flour
1 cup mashed potatoes	

Dissolve yeast in warm water and set aside. Scald milk, remove from heat, and stir in butter until melted. When cool, pour into bread bowl and blend in potatoes and eggs. Sift together sugar, salt, and 4 cups flour, and beat into wet ingredients, 1 cup at a time, to form a stiff dough. Add additional flour as necessary. Turn onto floured board and knead well. Place in buttered bowl, turn to grease top, and place in refrigerator until ready to bake. (Dough will keep 2 to 3 days. Punch down twice a day if not used right away.) About 1 hour before baking, pull off bits of dough, shape into rolls (see pages 114-116), and place on greased baking sheet. Cover and let rise until doubled. Bake in preheated 400° oven for 15 to 20 minutes.

Makes 2 dozen.

SWEET POTATO ROLLS

Special enough for a holiday dinner.

2 packages dry yeast
½ cup warm water
1 cup milk
⅓ cup sugar
2 teaspoons salt
1 cup cooked, mashed sweet
   potatoes

2 eggs
½ cup softened butter (1 stick)
6 to 7 cups flour
Melted butter

Dissolve yeast in warm water. Add milk, sugar, and salt. Blend in cooled sweet potatoes, eggs, and butter. Beat in flour, 1 cup at a time, to form a stiff dough. Turn out onto floured board and knead until smooth. Shape into a ball, place in buttered bowl, turn to grease top, cover, and let rise until doubled. Punch down and knead. Shape into rolls as desired (see pages 114-116). Place on greased baking sheet, cover, and let rise until doubled. Brush tops with melted butter. Bake in preheated 375° oven 20 to 30 minutes. *Makes 2-3 dozen.*

BUTTERMILK CRESCENT ROLLS

Basic dinner rolls that are terrific with stews.

3 to 3½ cups flour
2 tablespoons sugar
1 teaspoon salt
¼ teaspoon baking soda
1 package dry yeast
¾ cup buttermilk

¼ cup water
4 tablespoons butter (½ stick)
1 egg, beaten
Melted butter
Sesame seeds

Combine 1 cup flour, sugar, salt, soda, and yeast in large bowl. In saucepan combine buttermilk, water, and butter. Heat until butter melts. Cool and stir in egg. Beat mixture into dry ingredients. Add remaining flour, ½ cup at a time, to form a soft dough. Turn out onto floured board and knead until smooth. Place in ungreased bowl. Butter top, cover, and let rise until doubled. Punch down. Divide in half and roll both pieces into a circle about 12 inches across. Brush with melted butter. Cut each into 12 wedges; roll up, starting at the wide, outer edge, and place on ungreased baking sheets with points underneath. (Space 2 inches apart.) Curve to form crescents. Cover and let rise until doubled. Brush with melted butter and sprinkle with sesame seeds. Bake in preheated 375° oven 10 to 15 minutes. *Makes 2 dozen.*

TWO-DAY ROLLS

Just the thing for a busy cook, especially at holiday time.

1 package dry yeast	2 eggs
¼ cup warm water	½ cup melted butter (1 stick)
¾ cup milk	4 cups flour
½ cup sugar	½ teaspoon salt

Dissolve yeast in warm water. Stir in milk and sugar. Let stand at room temperature for 1 hour. Beat in eggs, butter, flour, and salt. Let stand overnight, not refrigerated. Divide dough into 2 balls. On floured board roll out each to ½-inch thickness. Cut each circle into 12 wedges. Roll up, starting at the outer, wide end. Place on greased baking sheet, seam-side down. Let stand at room temperature until doubled or time to bake (up to 12 hours). Bake in preheated 400° oven 10 minutes. *Makes 2 dozen.*

HOT CROSS BUNS

A traditional Eastertime treat.

1 package dry yeast	½ cup sugar
¼ cup warm water	1 teaspoon cinnamon
1 cup milk	1 cup currants or chopped
4 tablespoons butter (½ stick)	raisins
3 to 4 cups flour	1 egg, beaten
1 teaspoon salt	

Dissolve yeast in warm water and set aside. Scald milk, add butter, and stir until melted. When cool, combine with yeast. Sift together 3 cups flour, salt, sugar, and cinnamon. Beat dry ingredients into wet to form a stiff dough. Add more flour as necessary. Turn out onto floured board and knead in currants until they are evenly distributed through dough. Place in buttered bowl, turn to grease top, cover, and let rise until doubled. Punch down, pull off ½-cup amounts, and shape into rolls (see pages 114-116). Place on greased baking sheet. Cover and let rise again until doubled. Cut a cross in the top of each roll with a sharp knife, and brush top with beaten egg. Bake in preheated 400° oven 20 minutes. Cool, and frost cross with White Icing (see page 134). *Makes 1 dozen.*

HAMBURGER BUNS

Why buy these in the store when you can make your own?

2 packages dry yeast
1½ cups warm water
½ cup powdered milk
½ cup sugar

5 to 6 cups flour (unsifted)
2 teaspoons salt
4 tablespoons softened butter
(½ stick)

Dissolve yeast in warm water and set aside. Combine powdered milk, sugar, 5 cups flour, and salt in bread bowl. Blend in butter and slowly add yeast mixture. Beat until well mixed. Turn out onto floured board and knead until smooth. Add more flour if necessary. Place in buttered bowl, turn to grease top, cover, and let rise until doubled. Punch down, cover, and let rise 30 minutes (no longer). Using your hands, roll dough into a cylinder and divide into 12 equal pieces. Shape into buns and place on greased baking sheet, leaving several inches between them. Cover and let rise until doubled. Bake in preheated 375° oven 20 to 25 minutes.

Makes 1 dozen.

For Sesame Buns: Mix 3 tablespoons water with 1 beaten egg; brush mixture on buns and sprinkle with sesame seeds before baking.

CURRANT TWISTS

Use chopped raisins if currants are not available.

2 packages dry yeast
1 tablespoon sugar
¼ cup warm water
¾ cup sour cream or yogurt
1 egg

¼ cup milk
1 cup butter (2 sticks)
3 to 4 cups flour
1 cup currants
½ cup sugar

Dissolve yeast and sugar in warm water and set aside. Beat together sour cream, egg, and milk, and add to yeast mixture. Cut butter into 3 cups flour until crumbly. Add to yeast and sour cream mixture and blend to form a soft dough. Work in additional flour if needed. Shape into a ball and refrigerate overnight. Divide in half and roll out each piece ¼ to ½ inch thick. Sprinkle with currants and sugar, fold up, form into balls, and roll out again. Cut into strips 6 inches long, ½ to 1 inch wide. Tie into knots (see page 116). Place on greased baking sheet, cover, and let rise until doubled. Sprinkle with remaining sugar. Bake in preheated 375° oven 15 to 20 minutes.

Makes 3 dozen.

HAM AND CURRANT STRIPS

Serve as a party appetizer or for brunch.

½ cup currants
½ cup finely chopped ham
½ cup grated cheddar cheese
2½ cups flour
2 teaspoons baking powder

1 teaspoon salt
½ teaspoon baking soda
1 teaspoon dry mustard
⅔ cup milk
Melted butter

Preheat oven to 450°. Mix together currants, ham, and cheese. Sift together dry ingredients. Add milk and stir in currant and ham mixture. Blend well. Roll out into 8x12-inch rectangle, ½ inch thick. Cut into 1x3-inch strips. Place on generously buttered baking sheet and brush with melted butter. Bake 15 to 20 minutes.

Makes 28-32.

CORNMEAL ROLLS

Slightly chewy with a good corn flavor.

1½ cups flour
¾ cup cornmeal
4 teaspoons baking powder
¼ teaspoon baking soda
1 teaspoon salt

4 tablespoons butter (½ stick)
1 egg, beaten
¾ cup buttermilk
Melted butter

Preheat oven to 475°. Sift together dry ingredients. Cut in butter. Add egg and buttermilk, and beat. Turn dough onto floured board and knead gently for 3 minutes. Roll out to ½-inch thickness and cut into rounds with cookie cutter or rim of a glass. Place on greased baking sheet. Brush tops with melted butter and fold in halves. Bake 12 to 15 minutes.

Makes 12-15.

RYE ROLLS

Old-fashioned, moist rolls that are simple to make.

1 cup flour
3 cups rye flour
1 teaspoon salt

1 tablespoon baking powder
1½ cups milk
1 tablespoon melted butter

Preheat oven to 475°. Sift together flours, salt, and baking powder. Blend in milk and butter to form a smooth dough. Turn out onto floured board and knead briefly. Shape into 12 balls, place in greased muffin pans, and let sit 20 minutes. Bake 15 to 20 minutes.

Makes 1 dozen.

SHAPING ROLLS

Part of the fun of making your own rolls comes from the many choices you have in preparing the dough for baking. Here are a few of the possibilities. Shape dough as directed and place 2 inches apart on greased baking sheets, seam-side down. Cover, let rise, and bake in a preheated oven, according to recipe instructions.

Basic Rolls. Shape dough into balls, pat tops to flatten slightly. Or, make into ovals and flatten tops.

Cloverleaves. Roll dough into small balls, about the size of nickels. Place 3 balls in each section of greased muffin pan.

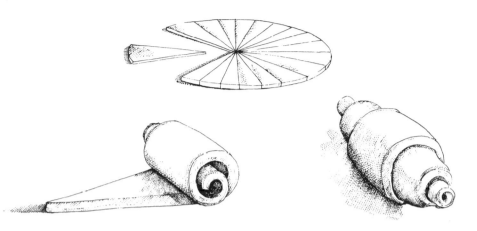

Crescents. Shape dough into balls and roll out into a circle ¼ to ½ inch thick. Cut into wedges (after cutting, dough will resemble a wagon wheel). Starting at the wide, outer edge, roll each piece up and place on baking sheet with points underneath. Gently curve each piece into crescent shape.

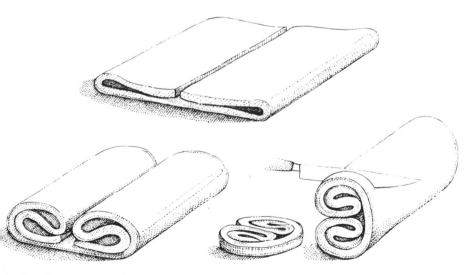

Palm Leaves. Roll dough into rectangle ¼ inch thick. Fold short sides in to center (to resemble a book jacket) and then repeat twice, forming a folded roll. Cut slices ¼ inch thick.

Stars. Shape dough into balls that will half fill greased muffin pans. With a pair of sharp scissors, cut north and south across the top of each ball. Make a second cut east and west, dividing each roll into four pointed sections.

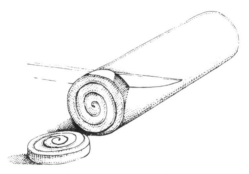

Swirls: Roll dough out into rectangle about ¼ inch thick. Then roll up rectangle tightly jelly-roll style. Cut into ¼-inch slices.

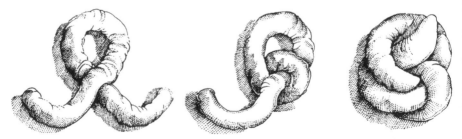

Twists. Roll strips of dough out into long, thin ropes. Form into "u" shape, cross ends, and form into a knot.

BASIC MUFFINS

Serve hot from the oven.

2 cups flour	1 egg
2 teaspoons baking powder	1 cup milk
1 tablespoon sugar	4 tablespoons melted butter
1 teaspoon salt	(½ stick)

Preheat oven to 425°. Sift together flour, baking powder, sugar, and salt. Beat together egg, milk, and butter. Stir into flour, mixing just enough to moisten dry ingredients. (Do not stir more than this.) Spoon batter into greased muffin pans, filling each ⅔ full. Bake 20 to 25 minutes. *Makes 12 large or 18 small.*

Muffin Variations:

To the sifted ingredients, add 1 tablespoon grated orange or lemon rind, plus 1 cup nuts, currants, raisins, or chopped dried apricots or prunes.

Or, add ½ teaspoon jelly to the top of each muffin before baking.

Or, add ½ teaspoon cinnamon and ½ teaspoon cloves to the batter.

Or, substitute 1 cup bran cereal for 1 cup flour.

SUNNY ALMOND MUFFINS

Divine for Sunday morning brunch.

1 package dry yeast	½ teaspoon salt
¼ cup lukewarm water	2 to 2½ cups flour
½ cup milk	2 eggs
⅓ cup butter	1 cup almonds, blanched and
5 tablespoons sugar	chopped

Soften yeast in water. Scald milk. Add butter, 1 tablespoon sugar, and salt. Cool to lukewarm. Add flour, beating thoroughly. Add softened yeast and eggs, 1 at a time, and beat until mixture is smooth. Cover and let rise until doubled in bulk, about 1 hour. Stir down and add ½ cup almonds. Fill greased muffin pans ½ full. Sprinkle with remaining almonds mixed with remaining 4 tablespoons sugar. Cover and let rise until doubled, about 30 minutes. Bake in preheated 375° oven for 15 to 20 minutes. *Makes 2 dozen.*

APRICOT TEA MUFFINS

Miniature upside-down cakes.

⅓ cup sugar
4 tablespoons butter (½ stick)
2 eggs
2 cups flour
3 teaspoons baking powder
1 teaspoon salt

⅔ cup milk
12 dried apricot halves,
   soaked in boiling water
   until soft
¼ cup brown sugar
2 tablespoons melted butter

Preheat oven to 400°. Cream sugar and butter until fluffy. Beat eggs separately and beat into creamed mixture. Sift together flour, baking powder, and salt, and add alternately with milk to creamed mixture. In each cup of a greased muffin pan, place one apricot half, cut side up; 1 teaspoon brown sugar; and ½ teaspoon melted butter. Fill cups ⅔ full with batter and bake for 20 to 25 minutes. Carefully invert onto serving tray and serve upside down. *Makes 1 dozen.*

CRISPY BACON MUFFINS

Bacon and eggs are baked right into this breakfast-in-a-bite muffin.

4 slices bacon
2 cups flour
2 teaspoons baking powder
½ teaspoon salt

2 tablespoons sugar
2 eggs
¾ cup milk
¼ cup melted bacon fat

Preheat oven to 400°. Fry bacon until crisp, drain, and crumble. Set aside. Into bowl sift flour, baking powder, salt, and sugar. In separate bowl, beat eggs and add milk and cooled bacon fat. Add to flour mixture all at once and stir until flour is barely moistened. Fold in crumbled bacon. Fill greased muffin pans ⅔ full and bake for 20 to 25 minutes, until nicely browned. *Makes 1 dozen.*

NORTHWOODS BLUEBERRY MUFFINS

Keep an extra dozen of these on hand in the freezer.

1 egg
1 cup yogurt
4 tablespoons melted butter
  (½ stick)
⅓ cup sugar

2¾ cups flour
3 teaspoons baking powder
½ teaspoon salt
1 cup fresh blueberries or
  frozen, thawed and drained

Preheat oven to 400°. Beat egg in small bowl and add yogurt. Add cooled butter and sugar, and mix well. Sift flour, baking powder, and salt into medium-sized bowl. Dredge blueberries in the flour. Stir egg mixture into dry ingredients and mix just until moistened. Fill greased muffin pans ⅔ full. Bake for 25 minutes.

Makes 1 dozen.

PRIZE-WINNING BLUEBERRY MUFFINS

A blue-ribbon-winning recipe developed by Dorothy Getchell of Old Lyme, Connecticut.

6 tablespoons butter
1¼ cups sugar
2 eggs, slightly beaten
2 cups flour
2 teaspoons baking powder
¼ teaspoon salt
½ cup milk

2¾ cups fresh blueberries, or
  2½ cups frozen, thawed and
  drained
3 teaspoons sugar
1 teaspoon nutmeg
1 teaspoon allspice

Preheat oven to 375°. Cream butter and sugar. Add eggs and mix well. Sift together dry ingredients and add to egg mixture, alternately with milk. Quickly fold in blueberries. (They must be well drained or muffins will be too moist.) Spoon batter into well-greased muffin pans until ¾ full. Combine sugar, nutmeg, and allspice, and sprinkle on each muffin. Bake 25 to 30 minutes. Remove from oven and immediately cover with a clean towel for 10 minutes, to prevent hard crust from forming. *Makes 1 dozen.*

CRANBERRY MUFFINS

Colorful, moist muffins to serve with any meal.

2 cups flour	2 eggs
½ cup sugar	1 cup milk
1 tablespoon baking powder	4 tablespoons melted butter
½ teaspoon salt	(½ stick)
½ teaspoon cinnamon	2 cups chopped cranberries

Preheat oven to 400°. Sift together flour, sugar, baking powder, salt, and cinnamon. Beat together eggs, milk, and butter. Add wet ingredients to dry and stir just until moistened. Fold in cranberries. Fill greased muffin pan ⅔ full and bake 25 to 30 minutes.

Makes 1½ dozen.

CHEESE MUFFINS

Attractive muffins that taste somewhat like biscuits.

2 cups flour	1 egg
1 tablespoon baking powder	1 cup milk
½ teaspoon salt	1 cup grated cheddar cheese
4 tablespoons butter (½ stick)	

Preheat oven to 425°. Sift together flour, baking powder, and salt. Cut in butter. Beat together egg and milk, and add to dry ingredients. Stir in cheese. Fill greased muffin pans ⅔ full and bake 20 to 25 minutes. *Makes 1 dozen.*

CORN MUFFINS

Similar to corn bread.

1½ cups flour	1½ cups milk
4 tablespoons sugar	1 egg
2 teaspoons baking powder	4 tablespoons melted butter
1 teaspoon salt	(½ stick)
1 cup cornmeal	

Preheat oven to 425°. Sift together flour, sugar, baking powder, and salt. Add cornmeal. Beat together milk, egg, and butter, and blend into dry ingredients, stirring just until moistened. Fill greased muffin pans ⅔ full and bake 20 to 25 minutes. *Makes 1 dozen.*

OLD-FASHIONED DATE MUFFINS

These are just as good as ever for breakfast or tea.

2 cups flour
½ teaspoon salt
2 tablespoons sugar
4 teaspoons baking powder
1 egg

4 tablespoons melted butter
(½ stick)
1 cup milk
¾ cup chopped dates

Preheat oven to 400°. Sift together flour, salt, sugar, and baking powder. In separate bowl, beat egg and add cooled butter and milk. Add all at once to flour mixture, and stir just until flour is moistened. Fold in dates. Spoon into greased muffin pans, filling them ⅔ full. Bake for 20 to 25 minutes. *Makes 1 dozen.*

GRAHAM MUFFINS

Bake in gem pans or muffin pans.

2 cups graham flour
1 cup milk
1 egg, beaten
1 tablespoon sugar

2 tablespoons melted butter
1 teaspoon cream of tartar
½ teaspoon baking soda
½ teaspoon salt

Preheat oven to 400°. If cast-iron pans are used, grease and place in hot oven. Combine all ingredients quickly, blending just enough to moisten dry ingredients. Fill greased pans ⅔ full and and bake 10 to 15 minutes. *Makes 1 dozen.*

HAM AND PUMPKIN MUFFINS

These are still tasty even when reheated several days after baking.

½ cup sugar
2 tablespoons melted butter
1 egg
½ teaspoon salt
1 cup pumpkin, canned, or
   cooked and mashed

2½ cups flour
2 teaspoons baking powder
½ teaspoon baking soda
1 cup chopped ham

Preheat oven to 375°. Beat together sugar, butter, egg, salt, and cooled pumpkin. Sift together dry ingredients. Toss in ham and blend until coated with flour. Stir into wet ingredients until just moistened. Bake in greased muffin pans 20 to 25 minutes.

Makes 1 dozen.

OATMEAL-RAISIN MUFFINS

With cocoa, a perfect snack on a brisk autumn afternoon.

1 cup quick oats	⅓ cup sugar
1½ cups milk	1 tablespoon baking powder
1 cup raisins	1 teaspoon salt
3 tablespoons melted butter	1 egg, beaten
1 cup flour	

Preheat oven to 400°. Combine oats and milk, and heat, stirring until blended. Add raisins and butter, and set aside. Sift together flour, sugar, baking powder, and salt. Blend oatmeal and milk mixture along with egg into dry ingredients, stirring gently. Fill greased muffin pans ⅔ full and bake 15 to 20 minutes.   *Makes 1 dozen.*

ORANGE MARMALADE MUFFINS

These are superb made with Dundee marmalade.

4 tablespoons butter (½ stick)	2 teaspoons baking powder
⅓ cup sugar	½ teaspoon salt
2 eggs	⅔ cup milk
2 cups flour	¼ cup orange marmalade

Preheat oven to 400°. Cream butter and sugar until fluffy. Beat eggs and beat into creamed mixture. Sift together flour, baking powder, and salt. Add alternately with milk to creamed mixture. Fill greased muffin pans ⅓ full. Spoon 1 teaspoon orange marmalade into each cup. Add remaining batter, filling each cup ⅔ full. Bake for 20 to 25 minutes.   *Makes 1 dozen.*

PEANUT BUTTER MUFFINS

An extra shot of protein for breakfast.

½ cup peanut butter, crunchy or smooth	1½ cups flour
¼ cup sugar	½ teaspoon salt
2 eggs, beaten	3 teaspoons baking powder
	¾ cup milk

Preheat oven to 375°. Cream peanut butter and sugar, then beat in eggs. Combine dry ingredients and add alternately with milk to peanut butter mixture. Fill greased muffin pans ⅔ full and bake for 15 to 20 minutes.   *Makes 1½ dozen.*

PECAN MUFFINS

Pecans and cornmeal give these little cakes substance and crunch.

⅓ cup sugar
4 tablespoons butter (½ stick)
2 eggs, separated
2½ cups flour
½ teaspoon salt

3 teaspoons baking powder
3 tablespoons cornmeal
1 cup milk
½ cup finely chopped pecans

Preheat oven to 375°. Cream sugar and butter. Beat yolks into creamed mixture. Sift together flour, salt, baking powder, and cornmeal, and add alternately to creamed mixture with milk. Beat until smooth. Beat egg whites until stiff and fold with chopped nuts into batter. Fill greased muffin pans ⅔ full and bake for 20 to 25 minutes. *Makes 1 dozen.*

RICE MUFFINS

Serve hot with butter and crabapple jelly.

1 cup cooked rice
2 cups flour
1 tablespoon baking powder
2 eggs, beaten

1 tablespoon melted butter
1 teaspoon salt
1½ cups milk

Preheat oven to 400°. Combine all but last ingredient, then stir in enough milk to make a fairly thin batter. Fill greased muffin pans ⅔ full and bake 20 to 25 minutes. *Makes 14-16.*

RYE MUFFINS

Light, and slightly sweet.

1 egg
1½ cups sour milk
½ cup sugar
1 teaspoon baking soda

½ teaspoon salt
1 cup flour
1 cup rye flour

Preheat oven to 400°. Beat egg and beat sour milk into it. Combine dry ingredients. Stir liquids into them, mixing until just moistened. Spoon into hot, greased muffin pans, filling each ⅔ full. Bake for 20 to 25 minutes. *Makes 1 dozen.*

YEAST MUFFINS

Keep a supply of these on hand in the freezer to complement any breakfast, lunch, or dinner.

1 package dry yeast	1 egg
¼ cup warm water	3 to 4 cups flour
2 cups milk	¼ cup sugar
1 tablespoon butter	½ teaspoon salt

Dissolve yeast in warm water and set aside. Scald milk, remove from heat, add butter, and stir until melted. Allow to cool and beat in egg. Sift together flour, sugar, and salt. Add yeast and milk mixtures, and blend. Cover bread bowl and let rise in warm place until doubled. Punch down and fill greased muffin pans ½ full. Cover and let rise again. Bake in preheated 375° oven 25 to 30 minutes.   *Makes 3 dozen.*

POPOVERS

Your oven must be very hot for these to succeed, so don't skimp on the preheating time! Expanding is caused by steam inside the crust.

3 to 4 eggs	1 cup flour
1 cup milk	1 teaspoon salt
2 tablespoons melted butter	

Beat eggs until light yellow. Add milk and butter. Beat in flour and salt until smooth, about 2 minutes at low speed of electric mixer. Fill greased custard cups ½ full and bake in preheated 425° oven 35 to 40 minutes. To assure crisp insides, stick a wooden toothpick into the side of each popover and bake 3 to 4 minutes longer.   *Makes 10-12.*

SPICY POPOVERS

Serve with butter for breakfast or as a dessert with your favorite sauce and whipped cream.

3 eggs	¼ teaspoon salt
1 cup milk	½ teaspoon cloves
3 tablespoons melted butter	½ teaspoon ginger
1 cup flour	

Preheat oven to 375°. Beat together eggs, milk, and butter. Sift together dry ingredients and beat into egg mixture. Fill 4 greased custard cups with batter, dividing it evenly among them. Bake 60 minutes.   *Makes 4.*

QUICK BISCUITS

With no kneading or rolling, these are simple biscuits for the cook in a hurry.

2 cups flour	4 tablespoons butter (½ stick)
2 teaspoons baking powder	1 cup milk
1 teaspoon salt	

Preheat oven to 450°. Sift together flour, baking powder, and salt. Cut in butter until mixture is crumbly. Add milk slowly, stirring with fork to form a soft dough. Drop by teaspoonfuls onto ungreased baking sheet and bake 10 to 15 minutes.   *Makes 1 dozen.*

For Rolled Biscuits: Follow previous recipe but cut milk back by about ¼ cup. Turn dough onto floured board and knead several times. Roll out ½ inch thick and cut with 2-inch round cookie cutter or glass. Place on ungreased baking sheet and bake 10 to 15 minutes.

ANNE'S BISCUITS

These have an unusual texture and a great taste.

½ cup butter (1 stick)	1 cup flour
1 cup brown sugar	1 cup fine bread crumbs
2 eggs	1 heaping teaspoon baking
½ teaspoon vanilla	powder
1 cup wheat germ	¼ teaspoon salt

Cream butter and brown sugar. Beat in eggs and vanilla, and dry ingredients. Mix well. Roll dough into cylinder 2 inches in diameter, place on baking sheet, and refrigerate overnight. The next day cut into slices about ¼ inch thick. Place on greased baking sheet and bake in preheated 350° oven 15 minutes or until brown.

Makes 2 dozen.

BEATEN BISCUITS

Float these cracker-like rounds in clam chowder or oyster stew; or top with cheese or ham.

2 cups flour	⅓ cup butter
1 teaspoon salt	⅔ cup milk

Preheat oven to 400°. Sift together flour and salt, and blend in butter. Add enough milk to make a stiff dough (amount will vary according to flour used and weather). Turn out onto floured board and beat with wooden mallet or rolling pin until dough blisters. Fold dough often as you beat. This should take about 20 minutes. Then roll dough out to ⅓-inch thickness and cut with a 2-inch cutter. Prick tops with fork, place on baking sheet, and bake about 15 minutes.

Makes 1½ dozen.

FRUIT BISCUITS

Use tart apples in this recipe.

2 cups flour	½ to ¾ cup milk
2 teaspoons baking powder	1 cup peeled, chopped apple
½ teaspoon salt	½ cup currants
2 tablespoons sugar	1 teaspoon grated lemon rind
4 tablespoons butter (½ stick)	

Preheat oven to 450°. Sift together flour, baking powder, salt, and sugar. Cut in butter until mixture is crumbly. Add milk slowly, mixing with fork to form a soft dough. Mix in apple, currants, and lemon rind. Drop by teaspoonfuls onto greased baking sheet and bake 10 to 15 minutes.

Makes 18-20.

HONEY RAISED BISCUITS

The dough for these biscuits can be kept in the refrigerator and used as needed.

2 packages dry yeast
½ cup lukewarm water
⅓ cup milk
⅔ cup butter
⅔ cup honey

1 cup warm mashed potatoes
1 teaspoon salt
2 eggs, beaten
5 to 6 cups flour

Dissolve yeast in water. Scald milk and add butter, honey, potatoes, and salt. Blend well. Cool to lukewarm and add yeast mixture and eggs. Add enough flour to make a soft dough. Knead for 10 minutes, wrap in wax paper or put in tightly covered bowl. Store in refrigerator and use as needed. Form dough into small balls that half fill a greased muffin pan, using three balls for each. Let rise until doubled in bulk. Bake in preheated 375° oven for 10 to 15 minutes.

Makes 4 dozen.

LEMON BISCUITS

Serve for breakfast or make in small tins for afternoon tea.

2 cups flour
2 teaspoons baking powder
½ teaspoon salt
4 tablespoons butter (½ stick)
2 teaspoons grated lemon peel

⅔ cup milk
3 tablespoons sugar
2 teaspoons grated lemon peel
½ teaspoon lemon juice
2 tablespoons melted butter

Preheat oven to 450°. Sift together flour, baking powder, and salt. Cut in butter. Add lemon peel and blend. Add milk and stir to form a soft dough. Turn onto floured board and knead several times. Roll out ½ inch thick and cut with 2-inch biscuit cutter or rim of a glass. Combine sugar, lemon peel, and lemon juice. Place half of biscuits in greased muffin pans, spread with melted butter and lemon mixture, top with remaining biscuits, pressing lightly together. Bake 8 to 10 minutes.

Makes 1-2 dozen.

HOT CREAM BISCUITS

Try dipping these in poppy seed or sesame seed before baking.

3 to 4 tablespoons butter
2 cups flour
4½ teaspoons baking powder

1 teaspoon salt
1 tablespoon sugar
⅔ cup heavy cream

Preheat oven to 425°. Melt butter and set aside. Sift together flour, baking powder, salt, and sugar. Using a fork, stir in enough cream to make a light dough. Transfer to floured board, sift a little additional flour on top, and pat the dough to ¾ inch thick. Cut with biscuit cutter, then dip each biscuit in melted butter. Arrange on greased baking sheet, and bake for 12 to 15 minutes.   *Makes 8 biscuits.*

POTATO BISCUITS

Use up leftover potatoes for these old-fashioned biscuits.

¾ cup flour
1 tablespoon baking powder
½ teaspoon salt

1 tablespoon butter
½ cup mashed potatoes
¼ to ½ cup milk

Preheat oven to 400°. Sift together flour, baking powder, and salt. Cut in butter. Stir in potatoes and milk, and blend with a fork. (Add more milk if mixture seems dry.) Spoon into 12 mounds on greased baking sheet and bake 15 to 20 minutes or until golden.

Makes 1 dozen.

RAISED REFRIGERATOR BISCUITS

Make dough ahead and store several days in the refrigerator.

3 packages dry yeast
½ cup warm water
⅔ cup milk
⅔ cup butter
½ cup sugar

1 teaspoon salt
1 cup mashed potatoes
2 eggs
6 to 7 cups flour

Dissolve yeast in warm water and set aside. Scald milk, add butter, and stir until butter melts. Add sugar, salt, and mashed potatoes; stir until blended and cool. Beat in eggs and add flour, 1 cup at a time, to form a stiff dough. Turn out onto floured board and knead until smooth. (If dough is not needed right away, store in covered bowl in the refrigerator. Punch down and knead several times each day it is stored.) To make rolls, place 3 small balls in greased muffin pans, filling them ½ full. Cover and let rise until doubled. Bake in preheated 375° oven 10 to 15 minutes.   *Makes 4-5 dozen.*

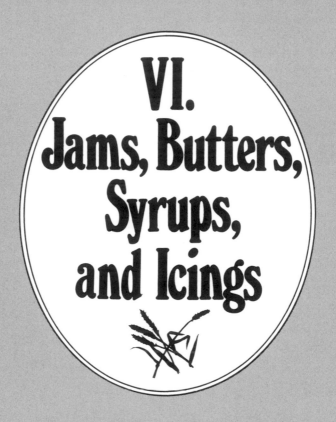

VI.
Jams, Butters, Syrups, and Icings

UNCOOKED JAM

This will not keep, so make only what you can use in two days.

1 cup cleaned berries (any kind)
1 cup sugar

Preheat oven to 325°. Pour berries in an oven-proof dish and sugar in another. Place containers on baking sheet and bake 20 to 30 minutes, until both are very hot. (Not all berries require exactly the same amount of time, so check periodically during cooking to prevent scorching.) Add sugar to berries and beat together until well blended. Pour into a dish or jar and cool before serving.

Makes approximately 1 cup.

CARROT-ORANGE MARMALADE

Serve on toast or muffins, or use in recipes that call for jam.

3 oranges
4 lemons
6 cups water

4 cups peeled, grated carrots
3½ cups sugar

Squeeze juice from oranges and lemons and set aside. Grate rinds and simmer in 3 cups water 20 minutes. Add carrots and remaining water, and simmer 15 minutes or until tender. Add juices and sugar, bring to a boil, reduce heat, and simmer 1 hour, stirring occasionally to prevent sticking. Pour into hot sterilized jars, leaving ¼ inch of headspace; seal and simmer 10 minutes in hot-water bath canner.

Makes 4 pints.

APPLE BUTTER

Use up right away, or process in boiling-water bath to lengthen storage time.

Follow your favorite recipe for applesauce, adding a bit more sugar for a sweet apple butter. Place hot applesauce in heavy baking pan and bake in preheated 250° oven until thick and dark. Stir occasionally during cooking to prevent sticking. Add cinnamon to taste and pack into hot, sterilized jars, leaving ¼-inch headspace.

SPICED APPLE BUTTER

Watch this carefully as it cooks so it doesn't scorch.

2½ quarts apples, washed,
  pared, quartered, and cored
1 quart cider vinegar
3½ cups sugar

¾ teaspoon cinnamon
½ teaspoon cloves
½ teaspoon allspice

Cook apples slowly in vinegar for about 1 hour, or until mushy. Add sugar and spices and cook until thick, stirring constantly. Turn into sterilized jars and top with paraffin when cool.

Makes 10 pints.

PEACH BUTTER

Makes a nice gift.

2½ pounds peaches, skinned,
  stoned, and sliced
1 pound sugar

1 teaspoon cinnamon
½ teaspoon nutmeg

Place peaches in heavy kettle, cover with sugar, and let stand 10 to 12 hours. Cook over very low heat, stirring frequently, until thick and soft. Press through food mill and add cinnamon and nutmeg. Pack into hot, sterilized jars, leaving ¼-inch headspace, seal, and process in boiling-water bath. *Makes 2 pints.*

PLUM BUTTER

No cooking is involved. Try this with other fruits as well.

2 plums, seeded
1 tablespoon honey
1 tablespoon molasses

4 tablespoons butter (½ stick)
1 teaspoon cinnamon

Combine all ingredients in blender and mix at medium speed until smooth. *Makes about ½ cup.*

CASHEW BUTTER

A special kind of spread.

1 cup chopped cashews
2 tablespoons peanut oil
1 tablespoon honey

Combine all ingredients in blender and mix at medium speed until smooth. Add more oil if mixture seems dry. *Makes about 1 cup.*

HERB BUTTER

Use in sandwiches, or on top of hot rolls and biscuits.

4 tablespoons softened butter (½ stick)
1 tablespoon chopped fresh herb (1 teaspoon dry)

½ teaspoon lemon juice

Combine above ingredients and mix well. Store in covered container in the refrigerator. *Makes ¼ cup.*

HERB SPREAD

Serve with any bread or rolls.

½ cup softened butter (1 stick)
3 tablespoons minced shallots

2 tablespoons minced parsley, chervil, or other herbs

Cream all ingredients and chill at least 2 hours before using. *Makes ½ cup.*

HERB HONEY

Strain into a fancy jar, and present as a gift.

½ cup herb leaves (mint, sage, thyme, or a combination of these or others)
2 cups honey

Gently bruise herbs with a wooden spoon and place in bottom of small saucepan. Add honey and heat gently for 5 minutes. Pour into sterilized jars and seal. Let stand in warm place for 1 to 2 weeks. Strain out herbs and serve. *Makes 1 pint.*

ORANGE-BUTTER SYRUP

Divine with fritters, pancakes, and waffles.

1 cup orange juice
1 tablespoon lime juice

¼ cup sugar
4 tablespoons butter (½ stick)

Combine juices and sugar in saucepan and heat to a boil. Add butter, reduce heat, and simmer until butter melts. *Makes 1½ cups.*

SPICED SYRUP

Serve warm on waffles, pancakes, or biscuits.

½ cup butter (1 stick)   1 teaspoon cinnamon
1½ cups maple syrup   ½ teaspoon nutmeg

Combine all ingredients, bring to a boil, reduce heat, and simmer 5 minutes.   *Makes 2 cups.*

ALMOND ICING

Especially tasty on sweet rolls, coffee cakes, and pastries made with cherries or cranberries.

1 cup powdered sugar
2 tablespoons water
1 teaspoon almond extract

Sift sugar, then add water and almond extract, mixing until smooth. If icing is thick, add more water, a few drops at a time, until thinner consistency.   *Makes 1 cup.*

WHITE ICING

A simple frosting for sweet breads, coffee cakes, and rolls.

2 cups powdered sugar
2 tablespoons warm milk
1 teaspoon vanilla

Sift sugar, add milk and vanilla, and blend until smooth. For a thicker or thinner icing, adjust amount of milk used. For colored icing, add a drop or two of food coloring.   *Makes 2 cups.*

FRUIT GLAZE FOR COFFEE CAKES

Allow pastry to cool slightly before adding the glaze.

Combine ½ cup jam or jelly with 2 tablespoons water and bring to a boil. Press through strainer. Brush on freshly baked pastry.
                                                                    Makes ½ cup.

Index